LAMDA
ANTHOLOGY OF VERSE AND PROSE
VOLUME XV

Introduction by Andrew Motion

PUBLISHED BY
OBERON BOOKS
FOR THE LONDON ACADEMY OF MUSIC
AND DRAMATIC ART

This edition first published in 1999 for the London Academy of
Music and Dramatic Art by Oberon Books Ltd
(incorporating Absolute Classics)
521 Caledonian Road, London N7 9RH
Tel: 020 7607 3637 / Fax: 020 7607 3629
e-mail: oberon.books@btinternet.com

A catalogue record for this book is available from the British Library.

ISBN 1 84002 120 9

Cover design for LAMDA by Society.

Printed in Great Britain by MPG Ltd, Bodmin.

ACKNOWLEDGEMENTS

For permission to reprint the copyright material in this anthology we
make grateful acknowledgement to the following authors, publishers
and executors:

Adams, Neil: copyright holder not traced; Angelou, Maya: *Caged
Bird* from *The Complete Collected Poems* by Maya Angelou
published by Virago Press; Arasanayagam, Jean: *Nallur* by permis-
sion of Forest Books Ltd; Asch, Frank: copyright holder not traced;
Atkinson, Kate: extract from *Behind The Scenes At The Museum* ©
Kate Atkinson, 1995. Published by Doubleday, a division of
Transworld Publishers Ltd. All rights reserved; Atwood, Margaret:
You Begin from *Poems 1976 - 1986* by Margaret Atwood published
by Virago Press; Barford, Wanda: copyright holder not traced;
Barrie, J. M.: copyright holder not traced; Baxter, James K.: copy-
right holder not traced; Bennett, Alan: from *Writing Home* published
by Faber & Faber Ltd; Bennett, Rodney: copyright holder not
traced; Benson, Catherine: by permission of the author; Benson, E.
F.: extract from *Lucia In London* reprinted by kind permission of A.
P. Watt Ltd; Bergman, Ingmar: extract from *The Magic Lantern: an
autobiography* translated by Joan Tate, published by Hamish
Hamilton, 1988 © Ingmar Bergman, 1987. This translation © Joan
Tate, 1988; de Bernière, Louis: extract from *Captain Corelli's Man-
dolin* published by Secker & Warburg by permission of Random
House UK Ltd; Berry, James: *Watching A Dancer* from *Playing A
Dazzler* (p44, 21 lines) by James Berry (Hamish Hamilton, 1996) ©
James Berry, 1996; Bowen, Elizabeth: extract from *The Last September* © Elizabeth Bowen, 1929, 1952, reproduced by permission of
Curtis Brown Ltd, London; Bradman, Tony: *Bullrod the Bulldog*
from *Smile Please* (p61, 20 lines) by Tony Bradman (Viking Kestrel,
1987) © Tony Bradman, 1987; Brownjohn, Alan: copyright holder not
traced; Burgess Mark: copyright holder not traced; Carroll, Lewis:
copyright holder not traced; Causley, Charles: from *Collected Poems*
published by Macmillan, by permission of David Higham Associates; Cavafy, C. P.: *Waiting For The Barbarians* from *The Complete
Poems of Cavafy* translated by Rae Dalven, published by Hogarth
Press, by permission of Random House UK Ltd; Chesterman, Hugh:
copyright holder not traced; Chute, Marchette: copyright holder not

Margaret: copyright holder not traced; Frost, Robert: *Two Look At Two* from *The Poetry of Robert Frost* edited by Edward Connery Lathem published by Jonathan Cape by permission of Random House UK Ltd; Fuller, John: copyright holder not traced; Fyleman, Rose: copyright holder not traced; Gaarder, Jostein: extract from *Sophie's World* published by Orion Children's Books; Gallico, Paul: *Speech* © Paul Gallico and Mathemata Anstalt, by permission of Gillon Aitken Associates; Gavin, Jamila: extract from *The Wheel of Surya* © Jamila Gavin, 1992, published by Methuen Children's Books Ltd, by permission of David Higham Associates Ltd; Gilman, S.: copyright holder not traced; Godden, Rumer: extract from *Premlata and the Festival of Lights* published by Macmillan, 1996; Golding, William: extract from *Lord of the Flies* published by Faber & Faber Ltd; Grahame, Kenneth: extract from *The Wind in the Willows* © The University Chest, Oxford, reproduced by permission of Curtis Brown Ltd, London; Graves, Robert: *Hide and Seek* from *Complete Poems* published by Carcanet Press Ltd; Greene, Graham: extract from *Our Man in Havana* published by Penguin, by permission of David Higham Associates; Hammond, Linda: *At the Supermarket* from *Five Furry Teddy Bears* (p78, 14 lines), Penguin, 1990 © Linda Hammond, 1990; Harrison, Gregory: copyright holder not traced; Heaney, Seamus: *Mycenae* unpublished but reproduced by kind permission of Faber & Faber Ltd on behalf of the author; Hesketh, Phoebe: copyright holder not traced; Hiçyilmaz, Gaye: extract from *Watching the Watcher* published by Faber & Faber Ltd; Hill, Susan: copyright holder not traced; Holder, Julie: copyright holder not traced; Hope, A. D.: copyright holder not traced; Hughes, Ted: extract from *The Iron Woman* published by Faber & Faber Ltd, and extract from *Tales From Ovid* published by Faber & Faber Ltd; Ireson, Barbara: copyright holder not traced; Kafka, Franz: extract from *Metamorphosis* published by Secker & Warburg, by permission of Random House UK Ltd; Katz, Bobbi: *Morning Song* from *Poems for Small Friend* © 1989, Random House UK Ltd, reprinted with permission of Bobbi Katz; Keane, Molly: from *Good Behaviour* by permission of Andre Deutsch Ltd on behalf of the author; Kenward, Jean: *Paint on my Finger* reprinted by permission of the author; King, P.: copyright holder not traced; King-Smith, Dick: extract from *The Sheep-Pig* published by Victor Gollancz/Hamish Hamilton, 1983 © Dick King-Smith, 1983; Kingsbury, Phyllis: copyright holder not traced; Laird, Elizabeth: from *Red Sky In The Morning* © 1988, Elizabeth Laird, published in the UK by Heinemann Young Books, an imprint of

and the Sea of Stories published by Penguin Books, 1991 © Salman Rushdie; Russell-Smith, M. and G.: copyright holder not traced; Scannell, Vernon: *The Magic Show* by kind permission of the author; Serraillier, Ian: copyright holder not traced; Sitwell, Edith: copyright holder not traced; Slater, W. S.: *The Proper Study* reproduced by permission of Punch Publications; Smith, Stevie: copyright holder not traced; Steinbeck, John: copyright holder not traced; Storey, Edward: copyright holder not traced; Tagore, Rabindranath: copyright holder not traced; Taylor, Mildred D.: extract from *Roll of Thunder, Hear My Cry* published by Victor Gollancz / Hamish Hamilton, 1977 © Mildred D. Taylor, 1976; Thomas, Dylan: extract from *A Child's Christmas in Wales* published by Orion Children's Books, 1978; Thomas, Ruth: extract from *The Secret* published by Red Fox and by permission of Random House UK Ltd; Thubron, Colin: extract from *Behind The Wall* published by William Heinemann, by permission of Random House UK Ltd; Tolkien, J. R. R.: *Oliphaunt* by permission of George Allen & Unwin an imprint of HarperCollins Publishers Ltd © J. R. R. Tolkien; Turner, Steve: reprinted by kind permission of the author; Viorst, Judith: copyright holder not traced; Westall, Robert: extract from *The Machine Gunners* published and reproduced by permission of Macmillan Children's Books, London; White, E. B.: extract from *Charlotte's Web* published by Hamish Hamilton, 1952 © J. White, 1952; Wilson, Raymond: copyright holder not traced; Woolf, Virginia: extract from *A Room of One's Own* reprinted by permission of the Society of Authors as the literary representative of the Estate of Virginia Woolf; Yeats, W. B.: *The Wild Swans at Coole* by permission of A. P. Watt Ltd on behalf of Michael B. Yeats; Zabalotsky, Nikolai: *The Face of a Horse* from *Poems* by Nikolai Zabalotsky translated by Daniel Weissbort by permission of Carcanet Press Ltd; Zola, Emile: extract from *Thérèse Raquin* published by Oxford University Press World's Classics, translated by Andrew Rothwell, by permission of Oxford University Press.

Every effort has been made to trace the owners of copyright material but difficulties have arisen in a few cases of contested or transferred ownership. We apologise to anyone whom our enquiries did not reach and we invite them to apply to LAMDA for proper acknowledgement.

CONTENTS

INTRODUCTION

In the spring of 1914 the American poet Robert Frost was staying in Gloucestershire near his friend Edward Thomas. When Eleanor Farjeon came up to join them for a few days, the pattern of their time remained the same – an easy mixture of walking and talking – but the emphasis changed in their conversation. Where it had previously been exploratory now it was explanatory – especially in matters related to Frost's verse-theory of "the sound of sense". This theory, Frost maintained, was designed to prove that "the living part of a poem is the intonation entangled somehow in the syntax, idiom and meaning of a sentence. It is only there for those who have heard it properly in conversation. It is not for us (English speakers) in any Greek or Latin poem because our ears have not been filled with the tones of Greek or Roman talk. It is the most volatile and at the same time important part of poetry. It goes and the language becomes a dead language, the poetry dead poetry... Words exist in the mouth, not in books."

Thomas understood exactly what Frost meant, as his own poems (which he began writing later this same year) would soon demonstrate. Farjeon was not so quick on the up-take, and during one of their rambles around Ledbury she asked Frost to say more. Frost looked up, saw a man working in the fields nearby, and called a greeting to him. The man was too far off to hear precisely what was being shouted, but responded all the same – his own words also being a series of distance-muffled sounds. "There," said Frost triumphantly – and added that although the man was "inaudible", his intention was perfectly clear: it was a friendly reply. There was a meaning in sound, which underlay and informed whatever might appear in dictionaries.

Although Frost was thinking about poetry when he developed these ideas, his belief that "words exist in the mouth, not in books", is obviously important for prose too. It reminds us that the meaning of any well-written text is a compound thing – on the one hand articulate, self-aware, knowingly-shaped and full of accepted responsibilities; on the other hand, the opposite of all these things.

This is why LAMDA candidates, who are asked "to attain a good standard of speech", should feel they are involved in an excitingly complex task. They have to register the conscious-made aspects in whatever they are reciting, and at the same time release its unconscious forces. It is also why actors who perform words (especially poems) in a very actor-y way are immediately putting themselves at a disadvantage. They might have a beautiful voice. They might have fantastic control of the various elements which shape a passage (metre, punctuation, rhyme, rhythm, general architecture). They might give a wonderfully fresh delivery of the surface-sense. But unless they combine their expertise with a sense of what can never be mastered, they are only doing half of what is required of them.

Bearing this in mind, it is interesting to think about how poets themselves read their work. Ever since the first recordings were made towards the end of the nineteenth century, there have been people who made a virtue – and sometimes a great success – of reciting in flamboyant or theatrical ways. Think of Dylan Thomas – his great lilting wave-roll carrying into the furthest corners of public lecture halls. But these showpeople are exceptions proving a rule. Most of the poets whose readings we especially prize are those who – in any conventional respect – do not read particularly "well". Their intention is to honour what is visible and audible in their lines, but to purge them of glamour and razzle-dazzle and ostentation. They are focused on the secret resonance of their work, as well as its performative aspects.

Think of T.S. Eliot, with his astringent incantations. Think of Louis MacNeice with his flat nasal chant. Think of W.H. Auden

— his unshowy chat suddenly interrupted by the American "a" he adopted after leaving England in 1939. Think of Larkin, softly-softly swallowing his stammer. Think of Ted Hughes...

Well, yes, do think of Ted Hughes. Of all recent poets, he was the one who most magnetised listeners; his voice had an amazing Heathcliffian intensity, capable of sounding melting-tender one moment and savage-shocking the next, and often seeming to hover above the lines it spoke, like a hawk eyeing a kill, before stooping and speaking in one fell swoop. This was recitation in the Dylan Thomas class, and therefore apparently another exception to the general rule. Yet Hughes' performance never seemed irrelevant. Rather, it suggested the life that his poems led below their surface. Sometimes this life was delightful, sometimes it was dreadful — as he warned it might be. "Whether we approve or not," he once wrote, "we have to accept that when we recite verse or shaped prose, we invoke something. And what hears us, what approaches, is human spirit: closer and fuller human spirit. The question is: what is human spirit and is it a desirable thing?"

Where does that question leave anyone picking up this book, intending to use it for its express purpose? In a place which is filled with proper contradictions, that's where. It is a marvellously eclectic anthology, but everything in it proves the duality (at least the duality) of art. The best pieces tell us what we know as well as goading us towards knowledge of what we do not. They remind us of what is familiar while showing us what is strange. They console us by surprising us. They also make us remember (once we have decided to trust their excellence) that they are themselves the key to their own secrets.

Alastair Macaulay, the drama critic of the *Financial Times*, recently wrote a story which illustrates this. In conversation with Adrian Noble, the Artistic Director of the RSC, he drew from Noble an account of the actress Sam Bond rehearsing the great scene from *The Winter's Tale*, in which she, as Hermione, has to reproach her husband Leontes for falsely accusing her of adultery. Bond noticed that the line endings were "very weak" in her trial speech, but then she and Noble, "looked at the character's situation, working like Stanislavskians." She said: "I've given birth only 90 minutes before. Then the baby was taken away from me! And I'm being put on trial! And my husband thinks I'm an adulterer! And it's in public!" Accordingly, she broke the speech into deliberately awkward fragments – "Since what I am to say must be but that," and then quite separately, "Which contradicts my accusation and" – so as to give an impression of someone trying to gather their thoughts and keep control. And what did Noble think? "It worked wonderfully," he told Macaulay, closing the story with a phrase which all reciters should engrave on their hearts, "and it came purely from saying 'That's a funny line-ending.' It's a kind of phrasing that's worthy of Maria Callas. Genius phrasing. With Shakespeare, you come across these brilliant little points again and again – if you treat the form of the play as your best friend."

Andrew Motion
Poet Laureate

INTRODUCTORY

A LITTLE TALK

The big brown hen and Mrs Duck
Went walking out together;
They talked about all sorts of things —
The farmyard, and the weather.
But all *I* heard was: "Cluck!
  Cluck! Cluck!"
And "Quack! Quack! Quack!"
  from Mrs Duck.

Anon

MY SISTER LAURA

My sister Laura's bigger than me
And lifts me up quite easily.
I can't lift her, I've tried and tried:
She must have something heavy inside.

Spike Milligan

WHAT DO YOU SUPPOSE?

What do you suppose?
A bee sat on my nose.
Then what do you think?
He gave me a wink,
And said, "I beg your pardon,
I thought you were the garden."

Anon

A SPIDER BOUGHT A BICYCLE

A spider bought a bicycle
And had it painted black
He started off along the road
with an earwig on his back
He sent the pedals round so fast
he travelled all the day
Then he took the earwig off
And put the bike away.

Phyllis Kingsbury

LITTLE GREEN FROG

A little green frog in a pond am I;
Hoppity, hoppity, hop.
I sit on a little leaf high and dry
And watch all the fishes as they swim by –
Splash! How I make the water fly!
Hoppity, hoppity, hop!

Anon

SPLASH

"Splash," said a raindrop
　As it fell upon my hat;
"Splash," said another
　As it trickled down my back.
"You are very rude," I said
　As I looked up to the sky;
Then *another* raindrop splashed
　Right into my eye!

Anon

GROUP INTRODUCTORY

TADPOLES

Ten little tadpoles
  playing in a pool,
"Come," said the water-rat,
  "come along to school.
Come and say your tables,
  sitting in a row."
And all the little tadpoles said,
  "No, no, no!"

Ten little tadpoles
  swimming in and out,
Racing and diving
  and turning round about.
"Come," said their mother,
  "dinner-time, I guess."
And all the little tadpoles cried,
  "Yes, yes, yes!"

Rose Fyleman

AT THE SUPERMARKET

No stopping! No stopping!
We're doing the shopping.
There's lots of things to buy.
(Eggs) on the low shelves,
(Bread) on the middle,
and for (soap) we have to reach high.

No breaking! No spilling!
Our trolleys we're filling
with things we need today.

At checkouts we queue,
wait, pay and go through.
We then take our shopping away!

Linda Hammond

DINGLE-DANGLE SCARECROW

When all the cows were sleeping, and the sun had gone
    to bed,
Up jumped the scarecrow, and this is what he said:
"I'm a dingle-dangle scarecrow with a flippy, floppy hat.
I can shake my hands like this, and shake my feet like
    that!"

When all the hens were roosting, and the moon behind
    a cloud,
Up jumped the scarecrow, and shouted very loud:
"I'm a dingle-dangle scarecrow with a flippy, floppy hat.
I can shake my hands like this, and shake my feet like
    that!"

When the dogs were in the kennel, and the doves were
    in the loft,
Up jumped the scarecrow, and whispered very softly:
"I'm a dingle-dangle scarecrow with a flippy, floppy hat.
I can shake my hands like this, and shake my feet like
    that!"

M. Russell-Smith and G. Russell-Smith

JUNIOR PRELIMINARY

TOES

Toes,
handy to wiggle,
useful to kick;
fun to tickle,
hard to lick!
Good to count on,
walk on, run —
feet without toes
would be much less fun!
To me it's quite clear
there is nothing as neat
as a fine set of toes
on the end of your feet!

Judith Nicholls

IF YOU SHOULD MEET A CROCODILE

If you should meet a crocodile,
    Don't take a stick and poke him;
Ignore the welcome in his smile,
    Be careful not to stroke him.
For as he sleeps upon the Nile,
    He thinner gets and thinner;
But whene'er you meet a crocodile
    He's ready for his dinner.

Anon

SEAHORSE

O under the ocean waves
I gallop the seaweed lanes,
I jump the coral reef,
And all with no saddle or reins.

I haven't a flowing mane,
I've only this horsey face,
But under the ocean waves
I'm king of the steeplechase.

Blake Morrison

PAINT ON MY FINGER

Paint on my finger
   paint on my hair
paint on the end
   of my nose –
Why does the paint
   get everywhere?
Why, do you
   suppose?

Paint on my trousers
   paint on my shoes,
splatter and splodge
   and spot.
O, how I wish
   I had never begun!
O, how I wish
   I had not!

Jean Kenward

THE SNAIL

Have you ever seen a snail
Going off for walks
With his house on his back
And his eyes on stalks?
Well, when he has finished
He rolls them in his head,
And goes inside his tidy house
And tucks himself in bed.

Rodney Bennett

MORNING SONG

Today is a day to catch tadpoles.
Today is a day to explore.
Today is a day to get started.
Come on! Let's not sleep any more.

Outside the sunbeams are dancing.
The leaves sing a rustling song.
Today is a day for adventures,
And I hope that you'll come along!

Bobbi Katz

GROUP JUNIOR PRELIMINARY

THE SMALL GHOSTIE

When it's late and it's dark
And everyone sleeps... shhh shhh shhh,
Into our kitchen
A small ghostie creeps... shhh shhh shhh.

We hear knockings and raps
And then rattles and taps,

Then he clatters and clangs
And he batters and bangs,

And he whistles and yowls
And he screeches and howls...

So we pull up our covers over our heads
And we block up our ears and we STAY IN OUR BEDS.

Barbara Ireson

ANIMAL ACTIONS

Jump, jump, jump,
Like a big kangaroo,
Or the hunter will catch you
And send you to the zoo.

Wriggle, wriggle, wriggle,
Like a curly little snake,
Wriggle to the edge of
The great, green lake.

Now, be a robin,
Hopping, one, two, three,

Then spread your wings
And fly up to a tree.

Prowl, prowl, prowl,
Looking left and right,
Like a hungry tiger hunting
In the middle of the night.

Lie on the floor
And curl up very small,
Like a little hedgehog
Rolled into a ball.

Daphne Lister

THE BAND PASSES

One, two, one two one,
Bang! Bang! Beat that drum.
Clash! Clash! The cymbals go,
Beat them high, beat them low.

The Band is marching through the town,
See them pacing up and down,
Doors and windows open wide,
People peer from every side.

One, two, one two one,
Bang! Bang! Beat that drum,
Clash! Clash! The cymbals go,
Beat them high, beat them low.

Now they've passed along the street,
Quieter now the stamp of feet,
Into the distance goes the drum,
As windows close up one by one.

P. King

PRELIMINARY

LAZY WITCH

Lazy witch,
What's wrong with you?
  Get up and stir your magic brew.
  Here's candlelight to chase the gloom.
  Jump up and mount your flying broom
  And muster up your charms and spells
  And wicked grins and piercing yells.
   It's Halloween! There's work to do!
Lazy witch,
What's wrong with you?

Myra Cohn Livingston

BELLA HAD A NEW UMBRELLA˙

Bella had a new umbrella,
Didn't want to lose it,
So when she walked out in the rain
She didn't ever use it.

Her nose went sniff,
Her shoes went squish,
Her socks grew soggy,
Her glasses got foggy,
Her pockets filled with water
And a little green froggy.

All she could speak was a weak *kachoo*!
But Bella's umbrella
Stayed nice and new.

Eve Merriam

THE WRONG START

I got up this morning and meant to be good,
But things didn't happen the way that they should.

> I lost my toothbrush,
>   I slammed the door,
> I dropped an egg
>   On the kitchen floor,
> I spilled some sugar
>   And after that
> I tried to hurry
>   And tripped on the cat.

Things may get better. I don't know when.
I think I'll go back and start over again.

Marchette Chute

AIRLINER

I lie in the grass
And see in the sky
A moving spark
Ever so high...

Hard to believe
That, away up there,
Are ordinary people
Flying... where?

Perhaps to Bangkok,
Perhaps to Rome,
Some for a holiday,
Some going home...

Funny to think
That none of them know
That, away down here,
I'm watching them go.

S. Gilman

LEAF-FALL

Golden, yellow, brown and red,
Pirouetting overhead.
See them flutter, twist and curl
Dancing in a windblown whirl.
Till upon the ground they lie
With a brittle dying sigh,
Buried in the earth's warm bed,
Wrapped in coats of brown and red.

E. H. Ray

LET'S SEND A ROCKET

Ten, nine, eight...
Seven, six, five...

We'll send up a rocket,
And it will be *live*.

Five, four, three...
It's ready to zoom!

We're counting each second,
And soon it will boom!

Get ready for... *two*;
Get ready to go...

It's *two* – and it's – *one* –
We're OFF! It's ZERO!

Kit Patrickson

GROUP PRELIMINARY

WEDDING PROCESSION

Here comes the bridegroom,
Bride upon his arm,
Here comes the best man,
Putting on the charm,
Winking at the bridesmaids,
Dressed up very fine,
And trying to stop the little ones
From getting out of line.
Here come the mothers
In their fancy hats,
Walking with the fathers,
Having little chats,
Waving to the cousins,
The uncles and the aunts,
The grandmas and the grandads
And a man in stripey pants.
Here come the workmates,
Neighbours and the rest,
Friends of both families
In their Sunday best.
Here comes the parson
Walking up the aisle,
Click, click, the cameras,
Everybody smile – CHEESE!

Anon

THE SONG THE TRAIN SANG

Now
When the
Steam hisses;
Now when the
Coupling clashes;
Now
When the
Wind rushes,
Comes the slow but sudden swaying,
Every truck and carriage trying
For a smooth and better rhythm,
For a smooth and singing rhythm.

This... is... the... one...
That... is... the... one...
This is the one,
That is the one,
This is the one, that is the one,
This is the one, that is the one.

Over the river, past the mill,
Through the tunnel, under the hill
Round the corner, past the wall,
Through the wood where trees grow tall,
Then in sight of the town by the river
Brake by the crossing where white leaves quiver.
Slow as the streets of the town slide past
As the windows stare at the jerking of the coaches
Coming into the station approaches.

Stop at the front.
Stop at the front.
Stop... at the front.
Stop... at the...
Stop.
    AHHHH!

Neil Adams

THE FIREMEN

Clang! Clang! Clang!
Says the red fire bell —
"There's a big fire blazing
At the Grand Hotel!"

The firemen shout
As they tumble out of bed
And slide down the pole
To the fire engine shed.

The fire engine starts
With a cough and a roar
And they all climb aboard
As it shoots from the door.

The firemen's helmets,
The ladders and hoses,
Are brassy and bright
As a jug full of roses.

Whee! Whee! Whee! —
You can hear the cry
Of the siren shrieking
As they hurtle by.

At the Grand Hotel
There is smoke and steam.
Flames at the windows
And people who scream.

The biggest fireman
Carries down
A fat old lady
In her dressing gown.

When the fire is finished
The firemen go
Back through the same streets
Driving slow.

Home at the station
The firemen stay
And polish up the nozzles
For the next fire day.

James K. Baxter

GRADE ONE

THE SNOWMAN

Once there was a snowman
  Stood outside the door
Thought he'd like to come inside
  And run around the floor;
Thought he'd like to warm himself
  By the firelight red;
Thought he'd like to climb up
  On that big white bed.
So he called the North Wind, "Help me now I pray.
  I'm completely frozen, standing here all day."
So the North Wind came along and blew him in the door,
  And now there's nothing left of him
But a puddle on the floor!

Anon

THE INVISIBLE BEAST

The beast that is invisible
is stalking through the park,
but you cannot see it coming
though it isn't very dark.
Oh you know it's out there somewhere
though just why you cannot tell,
but although you cannot see it
it can see you very well...

Oh your heart is beating faster,
beating louder than a drum,
for you hear its footsteps falling
and your body's frozen numb.

And you cannot scream for terror
and you fear you cannot quell,
for although you cannot see it
it can see you very well...

Jack Prelutsky

THE MOUSE IN THE WAINSCOT

Hush, Suzanne!
Don't lift your cup.
That breath you heard
Is a mouse getting up.

As the mist that steams
From your milk as you sup,
So soft is the sound
Of a mouse getting up.

There! did you hear
His feet pitter-patter,
Lighter than tipping
Of beads in a platter,

And then like a shower
On the window pane
The little feet scampering
Back again?

O falling of feather!
O drift of a leaf!
The mouse in the wainscot
Is dropping asleep.

Ian Serraillier

RHUBARB TED

I knew a funny little man
His name was Rhubarb Ted;
They called him that because he wore
Rhubarb on his head.

I'd grown so used to this strange sight,
The cause I did not seek;
But then one day to my surprise,
I saw he wore a leek.

I asked him if he'd please explain,
And let me know the reason;
He said, "I'm wearing leek because
Rhubarb's out of season!"

Ann O'Connor

SUNFLAKES

If sunlight fell like snowflakes,
gleaming yellow and so bright,
we could build a sunman,
we could have a sunball fight,
we could watch the sunflakes
drifting in the sky.
We could go sleighing
in the middle of July
through sundrifts and sunbanks,
we could ride a sunmobile,
and we could touch sunflakes –
I wonder how they'd feel.

Frank Asch

BULLROD THE BULLDOG

I'm Bullrod the Bulldog,
I'm short and I'm fat,
I'm mean and I'm nasty –
Now how about that?

I snarl and I'm vicious,
I'm really quite mean,
I snap at the postman –
He always turns green.

But deep down inside me,
I'm really quite nice –
I might eat your cat,
But I'd never eat mice.

I might eat your mother,
But I'd leave you your dad.
Now how can a dog like
That be all bad?

But people don't like me,
I know it, I do –
But if I come round to your house,
You'll like me – WON'T YOU?

Tony Bradman

A CENTIPEDE

A centipede can run at great speed,
Because of his number of legs,
But when he hangs out his socks to dry,
It costs him a fortune in pegs.

A centipede likes to wear wellington boots,
But because of his centipede brain,
It takes such a time to sort out all the pairs
That he's never in time for the train.

A centipede has one hundred legs,
But I'm glad I haven't because
When the front of a centipede gets where it's going
His back end is still where it was.

Julie Holder

MOTORWAY WITCH

Here comes the witch.
She's not on her broom
But riding a motorbike
Going ZOOM... ZOOM... !

She's wearing a helmet
Instead of a hat
And there on the pillion
Is sitting her cat.

Please, no overtaking
For I should explain
With her speed-crazy cat
She prefers the fast lane.

She banished her broom
For that was her wish.
It wouldn't... ZOOM... ZOOM...
But only swish... swish!

Max Fatchen

GRADE TWO

GINGER CAT

Sandy and whiskered, the ginger cat
Sniffs round the corners for mouse or for rat;
Creeping right under the cupboard he sees
A little mouse having a nibble of cheese.

On velvety paws with hardly a sound
The ginger cat watches, and padding around
He finds a good hiding place under a chair,
And sits like a statue not moving a hair.

Then baring his claws from their velvety sheath
He pounces, miaowing through threatening teeth.
But puss is too late, for the sensible mouse
Was eating the cheese at the door of his house.

Mary Dawson

DOWN BY THE POND

> *I'm fishing*

Don't talk, anybody, don't come near!
Can't you see that the fish might hear?
He thinks I'm playing with a piece of string
He thinks I'm another sort of funny sort of thing.
> *But he doesn't know I'm fishing —*
> *He doesn't know I'm fishing.*

> That's what I'm doing —
> Fishing.

> *No, I'm not, I'm newting*

Don't cough anybody, don't come by!
Any small noise makes a newt feel shy.

He thinks I'm a bush, or a new sort of tree
He thinks it's somebody, but doesn't think it's Me!

And he doesn't know I'm newting –
No, he doesn't know I'm newting.
That's what I'm doing –
Newting.

A.A. Milne

WAKING

My secret way of waking
is like a place
to hide.
I'm very still,
my eyes are shut.
They all think I am sleeping
but
I'm wide awake inside.

They all think I am sleeping
but
I'm wiggling my toes.
I feel sun-fingers
on my cheek.
I hear voices whisper-speak.
I squeeze my eyes
to keep them shut
so they will think I'm sleeping
BUT
I'm really wide awake inside
– and no-one knows!

Lilian Moore

HIDE AND SEEK

The trees are tall, but the moon small,
  My legs feel rather weak,
 For Avis, Mavis and Tom Clarke
 Are hiding somewhere in the dark
  And it's my turn to seek.

Suppose they lay a trap and play
  A trick to frighten me?
 Suppose they plan to disappear
And leave me here, half-dead with fear,
  Groping from tree to tree.

Alone, alone, all on my own
  And then perhaps to find
 Not Avis, Mavis and young Tom
But monsters to run shrieking from,
  Mad monsters of no kind.

Robert Graves

WINTER MORNING

Winter is the king of showmen,
Turning tree stumps into snowmen
And houses into birthday cakes
And spreading sugar over lakes.
Smooth and clean and frosty white,
The world looks good enough to bite.
That's the season to be young,
Catching snowflakes on your tongue.

Snow is snowy when it's snowing,
I'm sorry it's slushy when it's going.

Ogden Nash

THE COLOURS LIVE

The colours live
Between black and white
In a land that we
Know best by sight.
But knowing best
Isn't everything;
For colours dance,
And colours sing,
And colours laugh,
And colours cry.
Turn off the light
And colours die.
And they make you feel
Every feeling there is
From grumpiest grump
To the fizziest fizz.
And you, and you,
And I know well
Each has a taste,
And each has a smell,
And each has a wonderful
Story to tell.

Mary O'Neill

THE SPANGLY DRAGON

The spangly dragon, he flies through the air,
He hasn't a worry, he hasn't a care.
He flaps high above on his bumbly wings
And with crumbly voice he joyfully sings:

"I'm the spangly dragon,
I'll weave you a spell,
I'll tell you a fib
And a story as well.
I'll eat all your gumdrops,
I'll drink all your fizz,
I'm the spangliest dragon
That ever there is."

On his bumbly wings he flies to the moon
And he nibbles away while humming this tune.
Then when he has finished, he's had his last bite,
The spangly dragon flies into the night.

Mark Burgess

SINCE HANNA MOVED AWAY

The tyres on my bike are flat.
The sky is grouchy grey.
At least it sure feels like that
Since Hanna moved away.

Chocolate ice cream tastes like
prunes.
December's come to stay.
They've taken back the Mays and
Junes
Since Hanna moved away.
Flowers smell like halibut.
Velvet feels like hay.

Every handsome dog's a mutt
Since Hanna moved away.

Nothing's fun to laugh about.
Nothing's fun to play.
They call me, but I won't come
out
Since Hanna moved away.

Judith Viorst

GRADE THREE

OLIPHAUNT

Grey as a mouse,
Big as a house,
Nose like a snake,
I make the earth shake,
As I tramp through the grass;
Trees crack as I pass.
With horns in my mouth
I walk in the South,
Flapping big ears.
Beyond count of years
I stump round and round,
Never lie on the ground,
Not even to die.
Oliphaunt am I,
Biggest of all,
Huge, old, and tall.
If ever you'd met me,
You wouldn't forget me.
If you never do,
You won't think I'm true;
But old Oliphanut am I,
And I never lie.

J. R. R. Tolkien

THE WIND

The wind is a wolf
That sniffs at doors
And rattles windows
With his paws.

Hidden in the night,
He rushes round
The locked-up house,
Making angry sounds.

He leaps on the roof
And tries to drive
Away the house
And everything inside.

Tired next morning,
The wind's still there,
Snatching pieces of paper
And ruffling your hair.

He quietens down and in the end
You hardly notice him go
Whispering down the road
To find another place to blow.

Stanley Cook

THE FALLOW DEER
AT THE LONELY HOUSE

One without looks in tonight
    Through the curtain chink
From the sheet of glistening white;
One without looks in tonight
    As we sit and think
    By the fender-brink.

We do not discern those eyes
    Watching in the snow;

Lit by lamps of rosy dyes
We do not discern those eyes
   Wondering, aglow,
   Fourfooted, tiptoe.

Thomas Hardy

SEAL-SONG

In a faintly blue-tinged crystal sea
a seal has turned to look at me,
deep-black eyes and body long,
it sings its own seal-song.

"Oh, keep my waters deep and fresh
and let there be many fish,
let all my friends swim next to me
this is a seal's true wish.

And keep the poison from the waves
and poison from the air,
let gulls and cormorants dive within
our waters, while we're there.

Let our friends, who live on land,
know the sea is deep and long,
and there is room for everyone
who can hear my own seal-song."

In a faintly blue-tinged crystal sea
a seal has turned to look at me,
deep-black eyes and body long,
it sings its own seal-song.

Robin Mellor

SPECIAL REQUEST

The day Mum had a record request on the radio
she was in the kitchen
putting the washing on.
We called her
and called her
and called her,
but all she said was,
"Turn that radio down!
I can't hear what you're saying."
So we shouted again
as loud as we could
and in the end she came
just as the record was finishing.
"That's my favourite song,"
she said.
"Why didn't you call me?"
So we explained.
She's still not sure whether to believe us
or not.
"Me?" she said. "Me?
A record for me?"

Brian Morse

NORMAN THE ZEBRA

Norman, a zebra at the zoo,
Escaped and ran to Waterloo
And caused a lot of consternation
In the rush hour, at the station.

He had an awful lot of fun
Chasing folk on Platform One,
And then he ran to Regent's Park
And hid there until it was dark,
And thought of his keeper, Mr Prout,
How cross he'd be, that he'd got out
So he tiptoes to the big zoo gate
And found he'd got there just too late.
Poor Norman had a little weep
And lay down in the road to sleep
And woke up early from his rest
With people walking on his chest.
And someone said, "I think that's new,
A zebra crossing by the zoo."
And with a snort of indignation,
Regretting leaving for the station,
He cried, "I've had enough of that.
How dare you use me as a mat.
I'm going straight home to the zoo."
He was just in time for breakfast too.

Jeremy Lloyd

THE PARK

I often wish when lying in the dark,
Snug as a mouse,
In my bed at the top of the house,
I was still playing in the park,
Lying there upon the grass
Beneath the sky
Watching clouds go by
Like faces in a glass;

I do not ever need to sing
Myself to sleep,
Try my hand at counting sheep,
Instead I ride the night air in a swing;
A comet flashing through the dark,
I fall asleep in the park.

Leonard Clark

I ASKED THE LITTLE BOY WHO CANNOT SEE

I asked the little boy who cannot see,
"And what is colour like?"
"Why, green," said he,
"Is like the rustle when the wind blows through
The forest; running water, that is blue;
And red is like a trumpet sound; and pink
Is like the smell of roses; and I think
That purple must be like a thunderstorm;
And yellow is like something soft and warm;
And white is a pleasant stillness when you lie
And dream."

Anon

GRADE FOUR

JENNY'S SONG

When I am old and grey, my dears
I shall live beside the sea
And bathe my feet in lemonade
and eat butter buns for tea.

And I won't give a tuppenny fig
For what the neighbours say
I'll go to bed at breakfast time
And night will be my day.

I'll dye my hair deep indigo
and clog dance all alone
and blow cadenzas at the clouds
on my battered sousaphone.

I'll eat custard tarts at midnight
And banana splits and fruit
And frolic in the ocean
In my favourite birthday suit.

I'll eat marzipan and ice-cream
And ride a motorbike
And dedicate my old grey years
To doing what I like.

Yes doing what I like, my dears
Each day a holiday
I can't wait until I'm old, my dears
So I think I'll start today.

Gareth Owen

MIDNIGHT WOOD

Dark in the wood the shadows stir:
  What do you see ? –
Mist and moonlight, star and cloud,
Hunchback shapes that creep and crowd
    From tree to tree.

Dark in the wood a thin wind calls:
  What do you hear ?
Frond and fern and clutching grass
Snigger at you as you pass,
    Whispering fear.

Dark in the wood a river flows:
  What does it hide ? –
Otter, water-rat, old tin can,
Bones of fish and bones of a man
    Drift in its tide.

Dark in the wood the owlets shriek:
  What do they cry ?
Choose between the wood and river;
Who comes here is lost forever,
    And must die!

                              Raymond Wilson

CHILDHOOD

I used to think that grown-up people chose
To have stiff backs and wrinkles round their nose,
And veins like small fat snakes on either hand,
On purpose to be grand.

Till through the banisters I watched one day
My great aunt Etty's friend who was going away,
And how her onyx beads had come unstrung.
I saw her grope to find them as they rolled;
And then I knew that she was helplessly old,
As I was helplessly young.

Frances Cornford

WATERWAY ROBBERY

A pike in the river
Had cornered a carp:
"Five pounds or your life
And you'd better look sharp!"
The carp gasped and bubbled:
"Five pounds! But I'm clean,
I don't carry money,
I haven't a bean."
The pike grinned: "No matter,
They say carp's quite tasty."
"Oh, give me a chance,"
Begged the carp, "don't be hasty;
Just wait here one minute
And, quick as a flash,
I'll go and come back
With the relevant cash."
"OK," hissed the pike.
"One minute you've got
To pay me before
Things start getting hot.
Now scram!" The carp did
And as fast as you like
Returned with a fiver

To pay off the pike
Who left with a swirl
Of his emerald flanks...
"Thank goodness," the carp thought,
"That rivers have banks !"

Richard Edwards

ESCAPE AT BEDTIME

The lights from the parlour and kitchen shone out
Through the blinds and the windows and bars;
And high overhead and all moving about,
There were thousands of millions of stars.
There ne'er were such thousands of leaves on a tree,
Nor of people in church or the park,
As the crowds of the stars that looked down on me,
And that glittered and winked in the dark.
The Dog and the Plough, and the Hunter, and all,
And the star of the sailor, and Mars,
These shone in the sky, and the pail by the wall
Would be half full of water and stars.
They saw me at last, and they chased me with cries,
And they soon had me packed into bed;
But the glory kept shining and bright in my eyes,
And the stars going round in my head.

Robert Louis Stevenson

WHO MADE THE WORLD?

Who was it made the world, Sir ?
A bang brought creation about.
Who set off the explosion, Sir ?
I don't know. They're still finding out.

Did this big bang make you deaf, Sir ?
It happened a long time ago.
How do you know it happened, Sir ?
A man in a book told me so.

Who was the man in the book, Sir ?
A man who looked up in the sky.
How do you know that he knew, Sir ?
Because I believe him, that's why.

Who was it made me and you, Sir ?
A creature crept out of the sea.
Who was it made the creature, Sir ?
The creature just happened to be.

Why did it creep from the sea, Sir ?
It thought it was time for a change.
How did it grow arms and legs, Sir ?
I know, it sounds awfully strange.

Where do we go when we die, Sir ?
Don't know, but I'm sure that it's great.
Who was it made the place great, Sir ?
No talking now children, it's late.

Steve Turner

BLIND ALLEY

There's a turning I must pass
Often four times a day,
Narrow, rather dark, with grass
Growing, a neglected way;

Two long walls, a tumbled shed,
Bushes shadowing each wall —
When I've wondered where it led
People say, Nowhere at all.

But if that is true, oh why
Should this turning be at all?
Some time, in the daylight, I
Will creep up along the wall;

For it somehow makes you think,
It has such a secret air,
It might lead you to the brink
Of — oh well, of anywhere!

Some time I will go. And see,
Here's the turning just in sight,
Full of shadows beckoning me!
Some time, yes. But not tonight.

Eleanor Farjeon

DISTRACTED THE MOTHER
SAID TO HER BOY

Distracted the mother said to her boy,
"Do you try to upset and perplex and annoy?
Now, give me four reasons — and don't play the fool —
Why you shouldn't get up and get ready for school."

Her son replied slowly, "Well, mother, you see,
I can't stand the teachers and they detest me;
And there isn't a boy or a girl in the place
That I like or, in turn, that delights in my face."

"And I'll give you two reasons," she said, "why you ought
Get yourself off to school before you get caught;
Because, first, you are forty, and, next, you young fool,
It's your job to be there.
You're the head of the school."

Gregory Harrison

CHARLOTTE'S WEB

"Salutations!" said the voice.

Wilbur jumped to his feet. "Salu-*what*?" he cried.

"Salutations!" repeated the voice.

"What are *they*, and where are *you*?" screamed Wilbur. "Please, *please*, tell me where you are. And what are salutations?"

"Salutations are greetings," said the voice. "When I say 'salutations', it's just my fancy way of saying hello or good morning. Actually, it's a silly expression, and I am surprised that I used it at all. As for my whereabouts, that's easy. Look up here in the corner of the doorway! Here I am. Look, I'm waving!"

At last Wilbur saw the creature that had spoken to him in such a kindly way. Stretched across the upper part of the doorway was a big spider's web, and hanging from the top of the web, head down, was a large grey spider. She was about the size of a gumdrop. She had eight legs, and she was waving one of them at Wilbur in a friendly greeting. "See me now?" she asked.

"Oh, yes indeed," said Wilbur. "Yes indeed!"

E. B. White

THE IRON WOMAN

The rumbling started again. And the voice came again: "Do?" Then again, louder: "*Do*?" Then, with a roar: "DO?"

And Lucy and Hogarth almost fell over backwards as the Iron Woman, in one terrific heave, got to her feet. Branches were torn off as she rose erect among the cedars. And her arms rose slowly above her head. Her fists clenched and unclenched, shooting her fingers out straight. Then clenched again. She lifted one foot, her knee came up, then:

BOOM!

Her foot crashed down. The whole hilltop shook and the sound echoed through her great iron body as if it were a drum. Again, her other foot came up − and down:

BOOM!

Ripping the boughs aside, her fists clenching and unclenching, her feet rising and falling, Iron Woman had begun to dance. There in the copse, in a shower of twigs, pine cones, pine needles and small branches, she revolved in her huge stamping dance, in front of the Iron Man whose eyes glowed bright gold. And she sang, in that deep, groaning, thundering voice of hers: "Destroy the ignorant ones. Nothing can change them. Destroy them."

Ted Hughes

FLOUR BABIES

Compared to that, loving a baby was a piece of cake. In a sudden rush of affection, Simon halted in his tracks, tugged the flour baby out of his bag, and sat down with her on his knee beside the canal.

"I'll tell you what I like about you," he said, staring into her big round eyes. "You're very easy to get on with. You're not like Mum, always telling me to put my plate in the sink, or shut doors more quietly, or pick my shoes off the floor. You're not like Gran, always telling me how much I've grown, and asking me what I'm going to do when I leave school. You don't want me different, like all my teachers do. You don't tease me, like Sue. And you don't run off and leave, like my dad."

Tucking her under his arm, he gazed out over the water.

"I wouldn't mind you being real," he said. "Even if it was more work. Even if you howled, and kept filling your nappies, and threw giant tantrums in shops. I wouldn't mind."

He peeped down at her, comfy and safe in his armpit, and pressed a finger where her nose would be, if she weren't just a bag of flour.

Anne Fine

THE SHEEP-PIG

Babe made his way into the stables, curious to meet this, the first of the animals that he planned one day to work with, but he could not see into the box. He snuffled under the bottom of the door, and from inside there came a cough and the sharp stamp of a foot, and then the sound of a hoarse complaining voice. "Wolves! Wolves!" it said. "They do never leave a body alone. Nag, nag, nag all day long, go here, go there, do this, do that. What d'you want now? Can't you give us a bit of peace, wolf?"

"I'm not a wolf," said Babe under the door.

"Oh, I knows all that," said the sheep sourly. "Calls yourself a sheep-dog, I knows that, but you don't fool none of us. You're a wolf like the rest of 'em, given half a chance. You looks at us, and you sees lamb chops. Go away, wolf."

"But I'm not a sheep-dog either," said Babe, and he scrambled up the stack of straw bales and looked over the bars.

"You see?" he said.

"Well I'll be dipped," said the old sheep, peering up at him, "no more you ain't. What are you?"

"Pig," said Babe. "Large White. What are you?"

"Ewe," said the sheep.

"No, not me, you — what are you?"

"I'm a ewe."

Mum was right, thought Babe, they certainly are stupid. But if I'm going to learn how to be a sheep-pig I must try to understand them, and this might be a good chance. Perhaps I could make a friend of this one.

"My name's Babe," he said in a jolly voice. "What's yours?"

Dick King-Smith

THE WIND IN THE WILLOWS

There was a long, long pause. Toad looked desperately this way and that, while the other animals waited in grave silence. At last he spoke.

"No!" he said a little sullenly, but stoutly; "I'm *not* sorry. And it wasn't folly at all! It was simply glorious!"

"What?" cried the Badger, greatly scandalised. "You backsliding animal, didn't you tell me just now, in there – "

"O, yes, yes, in *there*," said Toad impatiently. "I'd have said anything in *there*. You're so eloquent, dear Badger, and so moving, and so convincing, and put all your points so frightfully well – you can do what you like with me in *there*, and you know it. But I've been searching my mind since, and going over things in it, and I find that I'm not a bit sorry or repentant really, so it's no earthly good saying I am; now, is it?"

"Then you don't promise," said the Badger, "never to touch a motorcar again?"

"Certainly not!" replied Toad emphatically. "On the contrary, I faithfully promise that the very first motorcar I see, poop-poop! Off I go in it!"

Kenneth Grahame

PETER PAN

"Tinker Bell," he called softly, after making sure that the children were asleep, "Tink, where are you?" She was in a jug for the moment, and liking it extremely; she had never been in a jug before.

"Oh, do come out of that jug, and tell me, do you know where they put my shadow?"

The loveliest tinkle as of golden bells answered him. It is the fairy language.

Tink said that the shadow was in the big box. She meant the chest of drawers, and Peter jumped at the drawers, scattering their contents to the floor with both hands. In a moment he had recovered his shadow, and in his delight he forgot that he had shut Tinker Bell up in the drawer.

If he thought at all, but I don't believe he ever thought, it was that he and his shadow, when brought near each other, would join like drops of water; and when they did not he was appalled. He tried to stick it on with soap from the bathroom, but that also failed. A shudder passed through Peter, and he sat on the floor and cried.

J. M. Barrie

THE BORROWERS

"Why so quiet, child?" asked Mrs May one day, when Kate was sitting hunched and idle upon the hassock. "What's the matter with you? Have you lost your tongue?"

"No," said Kate, pulling at her shoe button, "I've lost the crochet hook..." (they were making a bed-quilt − in woollen squares: there were 30 still to do), "I know where I put it," she went on hastily; "I put it on the bottom shelf of the bookcase just beside my bed."

"On the bottom shelf?" repeated Mrs May, her own needle flicking steadily in the firelight. "Near the floor?"

"Yes," said Kate, "but I looked on the floor. Under the rug. Everywhere. The wool was still there though. Just where I'd left it."

"Oh dear," exclaimed Mrs May lightly, "don't say they're in this house too!"

"That what are?" asked Kate.

"The Borrowers," said Mrs May, and in the half light she seemed to smile.

Kate stared a little fearfully. "Are there such things?" she asked after a moment.

"As what?"

Kate blinked her eyelids. "As people, other people, living in a house who...borrow things?"

Mrs May laid down her work. "What do you think?" she asked.

Mary Norton

HARRY POTTER AND
THE PHILOSOPHER'S STONE

The snake suddenly opened its beady eyes. Slowly, very slowly, it raised its head until its eyes were on a level with Harry's.

It winked.

Harry stared. Then he looked quickly around to see if anyone was watching. They weren't. He looked back at the snake and winked too.

The snake jerked its head towards Uncle Vernon and Dudley, then raised its eyes to the ceiling. It gave Harry a look that said quite plainly:

"I get that all the time."

"I know," Harry murmured through the glass, though he wasn't sure the snake could hear him. "It must be really annoying."

The snake nodded vigorously.

"Where do you come from, anyway?" Harry asked.

The snake jabbed its tail at a little sign next to the glass. Harry peered at it.

Boa Constrictor, Brazil.

"Was it nice there?"

The boa constrictor jabbed its tail at the sign again and Harry read on: *This specimen was bred in the zoo*. "Oh, I see – so you've never been to Brazil?"

As the snake shook its head, a deafening shout behind Harry made both of them jump: "DUDLEY! MR DURSLEY! COME AND LOOK AT THIS SNAKE! YOU WON'T *BELIEVE* WHAT IT'S DOING!"

Dudley came waddling towards them as fast as he could.

"Out of the way, you," he said, punching Harry in the ribs. Caught by surprise, Harry fell hard on the concrete floor. What came next happened so fast no-one saw how it happened – one second, Piers and Dudley were leaning right up close to the glass, the next, they had leapt back with howls of horror.

Harry sat up and gasped; the glass front of the boa constrictor's tank had vanished. The great snake was uncoiling itself rapidly, slithering out on to the floor – people throughout the reptile house screamed and started running for the exits.

As the snake slid swiftly past him, Harry could have sworn a low, hissing voice said: "Brazil, here I come... Thanksss, amigo."

J. K. Rowling

GRADE FIVE

NOAH AND THE RABBIT

"No land," said Noah,
"There – is – not – any – land.
Oh, Rabbit, Rabbit, can't you understand?"

But Rabbit shook his head:
"Say it again," he said;
"And slowly, please.
No good brown earth for burrows,
And no trees;
No wastes where vetch and rabbit-parsley grows,
No brakes, no bushes and no turnip rows,
No holt, no upland, meadowland or weald,
No tangled hedgerow and no playtime field?"

"No land at all – just water," Noah replied,
And Rabbit sighed.
"For always, Noah?" he whispered, "will there be
Nothing henceforth forever but the sea?
Or will there come a day
When the green earth will call me back to play?"

Noah bowed his head:
"Some day... some day," he said.

Hugh Chesterman

GREY SQUIRREL

Noses against the classroom windows,
teacher standing behind us, we stare out
as a grey squirrel nimbles its way
over this field's million sodden leaves
on this damp November day.

The trees drip, the grass is dank,
the playground shines like plastic.
A bedraggled sun. All's still, still,
except for that squirrel now busy
at husks of beech nuts, nibbling his fill.

Suddenly he's bolt upright, sniffing,
and then gone, swarming up a tree trunk
like Spiderman scaling a vertical wall.
Now he tight-rope-runs along a branch
and leaps to the next tree, does not fall.

We return to our tables. Chairs scrape.
Teacher stands at the board, chalk poised.
No-one speaks. For a minute we secretly gloat
over the wonder of that squirrel
in leather gloves and grey fur coat.

Wes Magee

THIS MORNING MY FATHER

This morning my father looks out the window, rubs his
nose
and says: Let's go and saw up logs
me and you.
So I put on my thick blue socks
and he puts on his army vest
and he keeps saying: Are you ready are you ready
It's a snorter of a day just look at the trees
and I run downstairs to get my old bent boots
that everybody says go round corners on their own they're
so bent
and he comes in saying that his tobacco is like old straw

which means that he is going to smoke his pipe today
So he says to mum: we'll be back in an hour or two
which means not for ages
but mum doesn't hear, because we lumberjacks are out the
door

   in a flash

Michael Rosen

SEA-FEVER

I must go down to the seas again, to the lonely sea and the
   sky,
And all I ask is a tall ship and a star to steer her by,
And the wheel's kick and the wind's song, and the white
   sail's shaking,
And a grey mist on the sea's face, and the grey dawn
   breaking.

I must go down to the seas again, for the call of the
   running tide
Is a wild call and a clear call that may not be denied;
And all I ask is a windy day with the white clouds flying,
And the flung spray and the blown spume, and the
seagull's
   crying.

I must go down to the seas again, to the vagrant gipsy life,
To the gull's way and the whale's way, where the wind's
   like a whetted knife,
And all I ask is a merry yarn from a laughing fellow-rover,
And a quiet sleep and a sweet dream when the long trick's
   over.

John Masefield

THE WASP'S SONG

When I was young, my ringlets waved
And curled and crinkled on my head.
And then they said, "You should be shaved
And wear a yellow wig instead."

But when I followed their advice
And they had noticed the effect
They said it did not look so nice
As they had ventured to expect.

They said it did not fit, and so
It made me look extremely plain.
But what was I to do, you know?
My ringlets would not grow again.

So now that I am old and grey
And all my hair is nearly gone,
They take my wig from me and say,
"How can you put such rubbish on?"

And every time that I appear
They laugh at me and call me "Pig."
And that is why they do it, dear —
Because I wear a yellow wig.

Lewis Carroll

OLD MRS THING-UM-E-BOB

Old Mrs Thing-um-e-bob,
Lives at you-know-where,
Dropped her what-you-may-call-it down
The well of the kitchen stair.

"Gracious me!" said Thing-um-e-bob,
"This don't look too bright.
I'll ask old Mr What's-his-name
To try and put it right."

Along came Mr What's-his-name,
He said, "You've broke the lot!
I'll have to see what I can do
With some of the you-know-what."

So he gave the what-you-may-call-it a pit
And he gave it a bit of a pat,
And he put it all together again
With a little of this and that.

And he gave the what-you-may-call-it a dib
And he gave it a dab as well
When all of a sudden he heard a note
As clear as any bell.

"It's as good as new!" cried What's-his-name.
"But please remember, now,
In future Mrs Thing-um-e-bob
You'll have to go you-know-how."

Charles Causley

QUIETER THAN SNOW

I went to school a day too soon
And couldn't understand
Why silence hung in the yard like sheets
Nothing to flap or spin, no creaks
Or shocks of voices, only air.

And the car park empty of teachers' cars
Only the first September leaves
Dropping like paper. No racks of bikes
No kicking legs, no fights,
No voices, laughter, anything.

Yet the door was open. My feet
Sucked down the corridor. My reflection
Walked with me past the hall.
My classroom smelt of nothing. And the silence
Rolled like thunder in my ears.

At every desk a still child stared at me
Teachers walked through walls and back again
Cupboard doors swung open, and out crept
More silent children, and still more.
They tiptoed round me
Touched me with their cold hands
And opened their mouths with laughter that was

Quieter than snow.

Berlie Doherty

CONVERSATION WITH AN ANGEL

On my way to Sainsbury's
I met an Angel. He stood
relaxed, one foot and one wing
off the pavement, waiting
for me to pass. I stopped
to see if he needed anything: had he
lost his way? Could I help perhaps?
No, he lacked nothing, simply wanted
some contact with the world again;
he'd been human once and he sometimes
craved that bitter-sweet flavour...
Some angels were born − he explained −
others translated. Could I
become an angel? Was there a waiting list?
Not a chance for you, he laughed,
no-one who has seen
an angel can ever become one.

Wanda Barford

THE MACHINE GUNNERS

At this time of night, the last of the sunlight caught them, long after the rest of the earth was dark. When they were very high, they glowed so small and bright it was impossible to tell them from the first stars. But they were not that high tonight. You could see their silver sides and fat fins; they looked like flabby silver elephants, nosing this way and that in the light breeze.

And then, and then... Chas gasped. Black on the blue dusk from the east it came: black twin-engined, propellers idling like fans, soundlessly gliding slow and low. A German aircraft.

A moan broke from Chas' lips; not of fear, but frustration. "The gun!" But it was a mile away, in Bunty's Yard.

The plane drew nearer. Lower. A faint sighing came from it, a whistling of strings and wires, like a kite. It was a fighter, with four cannon in the nose. The fighter wobbled, the nose veered and the tiny black cannon-mouths pointed straight at Chas. A face without goggles looked down at him from the cockpit, from rooftop height and only a football pitch away.

"Get down!"

Robert Westall

WHY THE WHALES CAME

As the weeks passed, the pattern of questions and answers between us changed. It became clear he wanted to ask questions but not to answer them. At first he wanted to know everything about us, all about our families. He wanted to know how old they all were, what they looked like, where they lived and what they did. "Father builds boats." Daniel wrote one day.

"What kind of boats?"

"Gigs. Luggers. Anything."

"Building one now?"

"Fishing lugger — 14ft."

"Flower crop good this year?"

"Fair."

"Potatoes? Any blight?"

"Late crop. No blight."

And when the messages were longer the Birdman used bits of wood, even seaweed, to make his letters. But he always signed them 'Z.W.' in orange shells.

His appetite for news became more and more insatiable. For Daniel and me it was like having to describe the world to a blind man. He wanted to know everything people said, everything they did. It was after we had told him about Big Tim, about how much we hated him, that he first began to talk to us through his messages rather than simply to ask more questions. "Never hate anyone," he wrote. "Hate eats away at your soul."

Michael Morpurgo

PREMLATA AND THE FESTIVAL OF LIGHT

A big bird flapped across the road, startling her awake. It gave a screech, "Auk! Auk!", which sounded horridly across the fields. For a while she walked more quickly, flagged again and froze: by the side of the road two big, shining, yellow eyes were looking at her. She knew they were animal eyes and that they were watching her.

Could they be a jackal's? Do jackals eat children? She had heard them howling at night around the village but jackals hunt in packs and there was only one pair of eyes. Then she remembered a tale Ravi had told of a leopard that had been seen on the plain. "Leopards spring on you and maul you," Ravi had said. To go on down the road Prem would have to pass it. Her hands were damp, she could feel trickles of fright-sweat running down her neck. "Somebody! Somebody come!" but there was nobody. Kali! If only Kali would come out of the sky, with her four arms and her sword. "Kali, Goddess, help me," whispered Prem. Kali would not be afraid of ten leopards. "Kali, *please*", but maybe Kali was angry because she, Prem, had not bought the *deepas*. Nobody came.

Perhaps if I keep quite still, she thought, it will go away, but the eyes seemed to be coming nearer.

Rumer Godden

GOODNIGHT MISTER TOM

She sat ashen-faced and watched him unpack. When he had finished she spoke in a quiet and controlled manner.

"Now I'll ask the questions and you'll give me the answers and no backchat. Where did you get them clothes and boots you're wearin'?"

"Mr Oakley and Mrs Fletcher."

"You steal them?"

"No. They were presents."

"You begged."

"No, I never."

"Don't argue. I said you begged."

He took hold of the eggs, fruitcake, wine and bedsocks and slid them across to her.

"Those are your presents," he said.

"You begged those too, I suppose."

"No. I've got a present of me own for you," he added. It seemed spoilt now. His surprise. It had been Mister Tom's idea. He picked up two pieces of cardboard that were strung neatly together and untied them. Inside was a drawing. It was of the graveyard and the church with fields and trees in the background. He passed it to her.

"It's where I lived."

She looked at it.

"You steal this?"

"No."

Now she would be pleased with him, he thought.

"No. I drew it meself."

She looked at him coldly.

"Don't lie to me."

Michelle Magorian

THE INDIAN IN THE CUPBOARD

How had it happened?

It never occurred to Omri now that he had imagined the whole incredible episode this morning. The Indian was in a completely different position from the one he had been in when Patrick gave him to Omri. *Then* he had been standing on one leg, as if doing a war-dance – knees bent, one moccasined foot raised, both elbows bent too and with one fist (with the knife in it) in the air. Now he lay flat, legs apart, arms at his side. His eyes were closed. The knife was no longer a part of him. It lay separately on the floor of the cupboard.

Omri picked it up. The easiest way to do this, he found, was to wet his finger and press it down on the tiny knife, which stuck to it. It, too, was plastic, and could no more have pierced human skin than a twist of paper. Yet it had pierced Omri's finger this morning – the little mark was still there. But this morning it had been a real knife.

Omri stroked the Indian with his finger. He felt a painful thickness in the back of his throat. The pain of sadness, disappointment, and a strange sort of guilt, burnt inside him as if he had swallowed a very hot potato which wouldn't cool down. He let the tears come, and just knelt there and cried for about ten minutes.

Then he put the Indian back in the cupboard and locked the door because he couldn't bear to look at him any longer.

Lynne Reid Banks

MRS FRISBY AND THE RATS OF NIMH

Just as we reached the food it happened. All around us suddenly there was shouting. Bright, blinding searchlights flashed on, aimed at us and at the mound of food, so that when we tried to run away from it, we could not see where we were going. Between and behind the lights there were shadows moving swiftly, and as they came towards us I could see that they were men — men in white uniforms carrying nets, round nets with long handles.

"Look out!" cried Jenner. "They're trying to catch us."

He darted in one direction, I in another, and I lost sight of him.

We all ran — straight towards the men with the nets. There was no other way to run; they had us encircled. The nets flailed down, scooped, flailed again. I suppose some rats got through, slipping between the men and past the lights. I felt a swish — a net just missed me. I turned and ran back towards the mound, thinking I might hide myself in it. But then came another swish, and that time I felt the enveloping fibres fall over me. They entangled my legs, then my neck, I was lifted from the ground along with three other rats, and the net closed around us.

Robert C. O'Brien

HAROUN AND THE SEA OF STORIES

"Down the hatch," he cried courageously; unscrewed the cap; and took a goodly gulp.

Now the golden glow was all around him, and inside him, too; and everything was very, very still, as if the entire cosmos were waiting upon his commands. He began to focus his thoughts...

He couldn't do it. If he tried to concentrate on his father's lost storytelling powers and his cancelled Story Water subscription, then the image of his mother insisted on taking over, and he began to wish for her return instead, for everything to be as it had been before... and then his father's face returned, pleading with him, *just do this one thing for me, my boy, just this one little thing*: and then it was his mother again, and he didn't know what to think, what to wish – until with a jangling noise like the breaking of a thousand and one violin strings, the golden glow disappeared and he was back with Iff and the Hoopoe on the surface of the Sea of Stories.

"Eleven minutes," said the Water Genie contemptuously. "Just eleven minutes and his concentration, ka-bam, ka-blooey, ka-put."

Salman Rushdie

THE RED PONY

Jody was glad when they had gone. He took brush and currycomb from the wall, took down the barrier of the box stall and stepped cautiously in. The pony's eyes glittered, and he edged around into kicking position. But Jody touched him on the shoulder and rubbed his high arched neck as he had always seen Billy Buck do, and he crooned, "So-o-o, boy," in a deep voice. The pony gradually relaxed his tenseness. Jody curried and brushed until a pile of dead hair lay in the stall and until the pony's coat had taken on a deep red shine. Each time he finished he thought it might have been done better. He braided the mane into a dozen little pigtails, and he braided the forelock, and then he undid them and brushed the hair out straight again.

Jody did not hear his mother enter the barn. She was angry when she came, but when she looked in at the pony and at Jody working over him, she felt a curious pride rise up in her. "Have you forgot the woodbox?" she asked gently. "It's not far off from dark and there's not a stick of wood in the house, and the chickens aren't fed."

Jody quickly put up his tools. "I forgot, ma'am."

"Well, after this do your chores first. Then you won't forget. I expect you'll forget lots of things now if I don't keep an eye on you."

"Can I have carrots from the garden for him, ma'am?"

She had to think about that. "Oh – I guess so, if you only take the big tough ones."

"Carrots keep the coat good," he said, and again she felt the curious rush of pride.

John Steinbeck

GRADE SIX

WATCHING A DANCER

She wears a red costume for her dance.
Her body is trim
and shapely and strong.

Before she begins
she waits composed,
waiting to hear the music start.

The music moves her.
She hears it keenly. The music
pulses her body with its rhythms.

It delights her. It haunts her body
into patterns of curves and angles.
She rocks. She spins.

She stretches entranced. She looks
she could swim and could fly.
She would stay airborne from a leap.

Her busy head, arms, legs, all know
she shows how the music looks.
Posture changes and movements are

the language of the sounds, that
she and the music use together
and reveal their unfolding story.

James Berry

MISS WING

At the end of the street lives small Miss Wing,
A feathery, fluttery bird of a thing.
If you climb the street to the very top,
There you will see her fancy shop
With ribbons and buttons and frills and fluffs,
Pins and needles, purses and puffs,
Cosies and cushions and bits of chiffon,
And tiny hankies for ladies to sniff on,
And twists of silk and pieces of lace,
And odds and ends all over the place.
You push the door and the doorbell rings,
And the voice you hear is little Miss Wing's.
"Good day, my dear, and how do you do?
Now tell me, what can I do for you?
Just half a second, please, dear Miss Gay –
As I was saying the other day –
Now what did I do with that so-and-so?
I'm sure I had it a moment ago –
As I was saying – why, yes, my dear –
A very nice day for the time of year –
Have you heard how poor Mrs Such-and-such? –
Oh, I hope I haven't charged too much;
That would never do – Now, what about pink?
It's nice for children, I always think –
Some buttons to go with a lavender frock?
Why now, I believe I'm out of stock –
Well, what about these? Oh, I never knew –
I'm ever so sorry – now what about blue?
Such a very nice woman – a flower for a hat?"
And so she goes on, with "Fancy that!"

And "You can never tell," and "Oh dear, no,"
And "There now! it only goes to show."
And on she goes like a hank of tape,
A reel of ribbon, a roll of crêpe,
Till you think her tongue will never stop.

And that's Miss Wing of the fancy shop.

James Reeves

SPEECH

When I have things to say
I expect you to listen to me.
If you cannot understand what I am saying
That is your fault and your loss,
But at least be quiet when I am speaking
And try to comprehend
You who think yourselves so clever,
Who know languages of the people
Of the living world and the dead,
Why cannot you learn mine
Which is so simple
To express wants so few?
"In"
"Out"
"Hungry"
"Thirsty"
"Give me just a taste of what you are having."
"Something hurts."
"My ball has rolled under the divan; get it out."
"Stop doing whatever it is you are doing and pay more
attention to me."

"I like you."
"I don't like you."
If you can talk to the Arabs, the Chinese, the Eskimos
And read the hieroglyphics of the past, why cannot you
understand me?
Try!

Paul Gallico

THE DAFFODILS

I wander'd lonely as a cloud
That floats on high o'er vales and hills,
When all at once I saw a crowd,
A host of golden daffodils,
Beside the lake, beneath the trees
Fluttering and dancing in the breeze.

Continuous as the stars that shine
And twinkle on the milky way,
They stretch'd in never-ending line
Along the margin of a bay:
Ten thousand saw I at a glance
Tossing their heads in sprightly dance.

The waves beside them danced, but they
Outdid the sparkling waves in glee: –
A Poet could not but be gay
In such a jocund company!
I gazed – and gazed – but little thought
What wealth the show to me had brought.

For oft, when on my couch I lie
In vacant or in pensive mood,
They flash upon that inward eye
Which is the bliss of solitude;
And then my heart with pleasure fills,
And dances with the daffodils.

William Wordsworth

SKY IN THE PIE!

Waiter, there's a sky in my pie
Remove it at once if you please
You can keep your incredible sunsets
I ordered mincemeat and cheese

I can't stand nightingales singing
Or clouds all burnished with gold
The whispering breeze is disturbing the peas
And making my chips go all cold

I don't care if the chef is an artist
Whose canvases hang in the Tate
I want two veg. and puff pastry
Not the Universe heaped on my plate

OK I'll try just a spoonful
I suppose I've got nothing to lose
Mm... the colours quite tickle the palette
With a blend of delicate hues

The sun has a custardy flavour
And the clouds are as light as air
And the wind a chewier texture
(With a hint of cinnamon there?)

This sky is simply delicious
Why haven't I tried it before?
I can chew my way through to Eternity
And still have room left for more

Having acquired a taste for the Cosmos
I'll polish this sunset off soon
I can't wait to tuck into the night sky
Waiter! Please bring me the Moon!

Roger McGough

WHO KNOWS IF THE MOON'S...

who knows if the moon's
a balloon,coming out of a keen city
in the sky—filled with pretty people?
(and if you and i should

get into it,if they
should take me and take you into their balloon,
why then
we'd go up higher with all the pretty people

than houses and steeples and clouds:
go sailing
away and away sailing into a keen

city which nobody's ever visited,where

always
        it's
        Spring)and everyone's
in love and flowers pick themselves

                                E.E.Cummings

CAN IT BE?

Can it be, can it be
That beasts are of various bravery,
Some brave by nature, some not at all,
Some trying to be against a fall?

I saw a cat. Beside a lily tank,
Paved level with the grass, she stood, this cat,
Considering her leap.
Three times she backed for jumping, gathered tight
(So tight, thought landed her already over)
And did not jump. And then,
After a pause, as scolding humanly
"Not nervy, eh? We'll see."
She jumped. And what a jump that was!
Quite twice as long
And high
As it need be,
Now why
Did this cat jump at all, so force herself?
There was a path around the tank,
She could have walked.

Can it be, can it be
That beasts are of various bravery,
Some simply brave, some not, some taking thought
(Most curiously) to cast themselves aloft?

Stevie Smith

I CANNOT GIVE THE REASONS

I cannot give the reasons,
I only sing the tunes:
the sadness of the seasons
the madness of the moons.

I cannot be didactic
or lucid, but I can
be quite obscure and practic-
ally marzipan

In gorgery and gushness
and all that's squishified.
My voice has all the lushness
of what I can't abide

And yet it has a beauty
most proud and terrible
denied to those whose duty
is to be cerebral.

Among the antlered mountains
I make my viscous way
and watch the sepia fountains
throw up their lime-green spray.

Mervyn Peake

THE CALL OF THE WILD

And over this great demesne Buck ruled. Here he was born, and here he had lived the four years of his life. It was true, there were other dogs. There could not but be other dogs on so vast a place, but they did not count. They came and went, resided in the populous kennels, or lived obscurely in the recesses of the house after the fashion of Toots, the Japanese pug, or Ysabel, the Mexican hairless — strange creatures that rarely put nose out of doors or set foot to ground. On the other hand, there were the fox terriers, a score of them at least, who yelped fearful promises at Toots and Ysabel looking out of the windows at them and protected by a legion of housemaids armed with brooms and mops.

But Buck was neither house dog nor kennel dog. The whole realm was his. He plunged into the swimming tank or went hunting with the Judge's sons; he escorted Mollie and Alice, the Judge's daughters, on long twilight or early-morning rambles; on wintry nights he lay at the Judge's feet before the roaring library fire; he carried the Judge's grandsons on his back, or rolled them in the grass, and guarded their footsteps through wild adventures down to the fountain in the stable yard, and even beyond, where the padlocks were, and the berry patches. Among the terriers he stalked imperiously, and Toots and Ysabel he utterly ignored, for he was king — king over all creeping, crawling, flying things of Judge Miller's place, humans included.

Jack London

THE WOMAN IN BLACK

What I heard next chilled and horrified me, even though I could neither understand nor account for it. The noise of the pony trap grew fainter and then stopped abruptly and away on the marsh was a curious draining, sucking, churning sound, which went on, together with the shrill neighing and whinnying of a horse in panic, and then I heard another cry, a shout, a terrified sobbing – it was hard to decipher – but with horror I realized that it came from a child, a young child. I stood absolutely helpless in the mist that clouded me and everything from my sight, almost weeping in an agony of fear and frustration, and I knew that I was hearing, beyond any doubt, appalling last noises of a pony and trap, carrying a child in it, as well as whatever adult – presumably Keckwick – was driving and was even now struggling desperately. It had somehow lost the causeway path and fallen into the marshes and was being dragged under by the quicksand and the pull of the incoming tide.

I began to yell until I thought my lungs would burst, and then to run forward, but then stopped, for I could see nothing and what use would that be? I could not get onto the marsh and even if I could there was no chance of my finding the pony trap or of helping its occupants, I would only, in all likelihood, risk being sucked into the marsh myself.

Susan Hill

THE VILLAGE BY THE SEA

Lila shook herself guiltily and ran into the hut, Bela and Kamal staring after her in agony, knowing there was no money. But she came out with something in her hand and when she handed it over the girls saw what it was – the ring their mother used to wear when she was well and that she had taken off and kept behind the mirror on the shelf now that she was ill. It was of silver – rather blackened and twisted now, but still silver. The girls gave a little gasp of astonishment but the man merely snatched it out of Lila's hand, stared at it, then at them, tucked it away into one of his pouches and marched off towards his cow without a word of thanks.

He set off with her, alternately stroking the hide-drum to draw long, strange sounds out of it, blowing on his trumpet and calling, "Hari Om, Hari Om," into the sky. Birds flew up in fright, screaming and wheeling till he was out of sight and hearing.

The girls were left staring at the leaf-packets in their hands.

"What shall we do with them?" Bela and Kamal asked.

Lila clutched the one in her hand as if she wanted to tear it apart or throw it away. "What shall we do?" she cried. "We can't do anything — we have to listen to him. There's no hospital in the village we could take her to, and no doctor who would come. We have no-one but the magic man to help us. Magic!" she said fiercely and turned and marched into the hut to do what the man had told her to.

Anita Desai

JANE EYRE

Meantime, Mr Brocklehurst, standing on the hearth with his hands behind his back, majestically surveyed the whole school. Suddenly his eye gave a blink, as if it had met something that either dazzled or shocked its pupil; turning, he said in more rapid accents than he had hitherto used:—
"Miss Temple, Miss Temple, what — *what* is that girl with curled hair? Red hair, ma'am, curled — curled all over?" And extending his cane he pointed to the awful object, his hand shaking as he did so.

"It is Julia Severn," replied Miss Temple, very quietly.

"Julia Severn, ma'am! And why has she, or any other, curled hair? Why, in defiance of every precept and principle of this house, does she conform to the world so openly —

here in an evangelical, charitable establishment – as to wear her hair one mass of curls?"

"Julia's hair curls naturally," returned Miss Temple, still more quietly.

"Naturally! Yes, but we are not to conform to nature: I wish these girls to be the children of Grace: and why that abundance? I have again and again intimated that I desire the hair to be arranged closely, modestly, plainly. Miss Temple, that girl's hair must be cut off entirely; I will send a barber to-morrow: and I see others who have far too much of the excrescence – that tall girl, tell her to turn round. Tell all the first form to rise up and direct their faces to the wall."

Charlotte Brontë

THE HOUNDS OF THE MORRIGAN

"Oh drat it! We missed him!"

"Sssshhhh! They'll hear you," the one with the red hair replied, and then she sniggered. She looked back over her shoulder and shouted:

"I say! Are you alright?"

She dismounted from the pillion and walked back.

"Frightfully sorry, old bean. Let me help you up."

"It's alright. I can manage," said Pidge.

"He's able to stand by himself," Brigit said firmly.

"Nonsense!" said the woman. "I must assist you. After all, what are fiends for? I *beg* your pardon! What I meant was – what are *friends* for. Dear, dear, I really must learn to listen to what I say."

She leaned forward and grasped Pidge by the arm and jerked him to his feet. She closed her eyes and held him for a moment like one in a trance.

Before letting him go, she gave him a nasty, nippy little

pinch. She smiled at him and then she aimed and spat a tobacco spit over the roadside wall.

"My name is Breda Fairfoul," she said chattily. "This is my friend, Melodie Moonlight."

Melodie turned the bike round and purred back to where they stood.

"Why do you chew tobacco?" asked Brigit.

"Like to bite something that bites back. Puts me in a hot mood," she said. She smiled again.

Melodie Moonlight looked penetratingly at her.

"Well?" she said.

"Too late," said Breda Fairfoul. "Another moment in time, peradventure."

"Foiled then," commented Melodie Moonlight. "The question is — by whom?" She turned to the children.

"Do come home with us and have some tea," she said silkily.

Pidge thought that her voice sounded like a cat singing the death song of a mouse.

Pat O'Shea

ROLL OF THUNDER, HEAR MY CRY

Papa touched Mama's face tenderly with the tips of his fingers and said, "I'll do what I have to do, Mary... and so will you." Then he turned from her, and with Mr Morrison disappeared into the night.

Mama pushed us back into her room, where Big Ma fell upon her knees and prayed a powerful prayer. Afterwards both Mama and Big Ma changed their clothes, then we sat, very quiet, as the heat crept sticky and wet through our clothing and the thunder banged menacingly overhead.

Mama, her knuckles tight against her skin as she gripped the arms of her chair, looked down upon Christopher-John, Little Man, and me, our eyes wide awake with fear. "I don't suppose it would do any good to put you to bed," she said quietly. We looked up at her. She did not mean to have an answer; we gave none, and nothing else was said as the night minutes crept past and the waiting pressed as heavily upon us as the heat.

Then Mama stiffened. She sniffed the air and got up.

"What is it, child?" Big Ma asked.

"You smell smoke?" Mama said, going to the front door and opening it. Little Man, Christopher-John, and I followed, peeping around her in the doorway. From deep in the field where the land sloped upward toward the Granger forest, a fire billowed, carried eastward by the wind.

"Mama, the cotton!" I cried. "It's on fire!"

Mildred D. Taylor

THE DAYDREAMER

There was a movement, a stirring inside the cat, and from the opening in the fur there came a faint pink glow which grew brighter. And suddenly, out of William Cat climbed a, well, a thing, a creature. But Peter was not certain that it was really there to touch, for it seemed to be made entirely of light. And while it did not have whiskers or a tail, or a purr, or even fur, or four legs, everything about it seemed to say 'cat'. It was the very essence of the word, the heart of the idea. It was a quiet, slinky, curvy fold of pink and purple light, and it was climbing out of the cat.

"You must be William's spirit," Peter said aloud. "Or are you a ghost?"

The light made no sound, but it understood. It seemed to

say, without actually speaking the words, that it was both these things, and much more besides.

When it was clear of the cat, which continued to lie on its back on the carpet in front of the fire, the cat spirit drifted into the air, and floated up to Peter's shoulder where it settled. Peter was not frightened. He felt the glow of the spirit on his cheek. And then the light drifted behind his head, out of sight. He felt it touch his neck and a warm shudder ran down his back. The cat spirit took hold of something knobbly at the top of his spine and drew it down, right down his back, and as his own body opened up, he felt the cool air of the room tickle the warmth of his insides.

It was the oddest thing...

Ian McEwan

THE MAGICIAN'S NEPHEW

They came at last into a hall larger and loftier than any they had yet seen. From its size and from the great doors at the far end, Digory thought that now at last they must be coming to the main entrance. In this he was quite right. The doors were dead black, either ebony or some black metal which is not found in our world. They were fastened with great bars, most of them too high to reach and all too heavy to lift. He wondered how they would get out.

The Queen let go of his hand and raised her arm. She drew herself up to her full height and stood rigid. Then she said something which they couldn't understand (but it sounded horrid) and made an action as if she were throwing something towards the doors. And those high and heavy doors trembled for a second aas if they were made of silk and then crumbled away till there was nothing left of them but a heap of dust on the threshold.

"Whew!" whistled Digory.

"Has your master magician, your uncle, power like mine?" asked the Queen, firmly seizing Digory's hand again. "But I shall know later. In the meantime remember what you have seen. This is what happens to things, and to people, who stand in my way."

C. S. Lewis

GRADE SEVEN

EVACUEE

The slum had been his home since he was born;
And then war came, and he was rudely torn
From all he'd ever known; and with his case
Of mean necessities, brought to a place
Of silences and space; just boom of sea
And sough of wind; small wonder then that he
Crept out one night to seek his sordid slum,
And thought to find his way. By dawn he'd come
A few short miles; and cattle in their herds
Gazed limpidly as he trudged by, and birds
Just stirring in first light, awoke to hear
His lonely sobbing, born of abject fear
Of sea and hills and sky; of silent night
Unbroken by the sound of shout and fight.

Edith Pickthall

THE DESTRUCTION OF SENNACHERIB

The Assyrian came down like the wolf on the fold,
And his cohorts were gleaming in purple and gold;
And the sheen of their spears was like stars on the sea,
When the blue wave rolls nightly on deep Galilee.

Like the leaves of the forest when Summer is green,
That host with their banners at sunset were seen:
Like the leaves of the forest when Autumn hath blown,
That host on the morrow lay withered and strown.

For the Angel of Death spread his wings on the blast,
And breathed in the face of the foe as he passed;
And the eyes of the sleepers waxed deadly and chill,
And their hearts but once heaved, and forever grew still.

And there lay the steed with his nostril all wide,
But through it there rolled not the breath of his pride:
And the foam of his gasping lay white on the turf,
And cold as the spray of the rock-beating surf.

And there lay the rider distorted and pale,
With the dew on his brow and the rust on his mail;
And the tents were all silent, the banners alone,
The lances unlifted, the trumpet unblown.

And the widows of Ashur are loud in their wail,
And the idols are broke in the temple of Baal;
And the might of the Gentile, unsmote by the sword,
Hath melted like snow in the glance of the Lord!

Lord Byron

THE PROPER STUDY

Seated before her window Mrs Jones
Described the passers-by in ringing tones.
"Look," she would say, "the girl at Number Three
Has brought her latest boyfriend home to tea;
And, see, the woman at the upstairs flat
Has bought herself another summer hat."
Her daughter Daphne, filled with deep disgust,
Expostulated "Mother, really must
You pry upon the neighbours? Don't you know
Gossip is idle, empty-minded, low?"
And Mrs Jones would murmur "Fancy, dear!
There's Mr Thompson going for his beer."
Daphne, an earnest girl of twenty-three,

Read Sociology for her degree
And every Saturday she would repair,
Armed with her tutor's latest questionnaire,
To knock on doors, demanding "Are you wed?
Have you a child? A car? A double bed?"
Poor Mrs Jones would remonstrate each week,
"Daphne, I wonder how you have the cheek.
And then to call me nosey!" Daphne sighed.
"Oh, will you never understand?" she cried.
"Mere curiosity is one thing, Mother:
Social Analysis is quite another."

W. S. Slater

CONSCIOUS

His fingers wake and flutter; up the bed.
His eyes come open with a pull of will,
Helped by the yellow May flowers by his head.
The blind-cord drawls across the windowsill...
What a smooth floor the ward has! What a rug!
Who is that talking somewhere out of sight?
Why are they laughing? What's inside that jug?
"Nurse! Doctor!" "Yes; alright, alright."
But sudden evening muddles all the air —
There seems no time to want a drink of water,
Nurse looks so far away. And everywhere
Music and roses burnt through crimson slaughter.
He can't remember where he saw blue sky.
More blankets. Cold. He's cold. And yet so hot.
And there's no light to see the voices by;
There is no time to ask — he knows not what.

Wilfred Owen

'I AM'

I am — yet what I am none cares or knows;
    My friends forsake me like a memory lost:—
I am the self-consumer of my woes:—
    They rise and vanish in oblivion's host,
Like shadows in love's frenzied stifled throes:—
And yet I am, and live — like vapours tost

Into the nothingness of scorn and noise,—
    Into the living sea of waking dreams,
Where there is neither sense of life or joys,
    But the vast shipwreck of my life's esteems;
Even the dearest, that I love the best
Are strange — nay, rather stranger than the rest.

I long for scenes, where man hath never trod
    A place where woman never smiled or wept
There to abide with my Creator, God;
    And sleep as I in childhood, sweetly slept,
Untroubling, and untroubled where I lie,
The grass below — above the vaulted sky.

John Clare

WILD FLOWER

Our uncut lawn to me alone brings joy,
With shaggy dandelion suns, grass bound;
To me they are not weeds, do not annoy,
Each ragged clump of leaves with light seems crowned.
I cannot understand my father's haste
To weekend mow and sever every head;
Though pleasing him, it leaves a barren waste,

A bare expanse of green, where once was spread
An emerald carpet buttoned down with gold.
So it looks now, with here and there a cloud
Of softest grey as tawny heads grow old.
Unseen I pluck each clock and laugh aloud.
I know, of course, they do not tell the hour,
But breath-blown seeds will fall, take root... and flower!

Catherine Benson

MANHATTAN

HERE those of us who really understand
Feel that the past is very close at hand.
In that old brownstone mansion 'cross the way,
Copied from one that she had seen by chance
When on her honeymoon in Paris, France,
Mrs Van Dryssel gave her great soirées;
And in the chic apartment house next door
J. Rittenhaus the Second lived – and jumped,
The morning after General Motors slumped,
Down from a love-nest on the thirtieth floor.
Tread softly then, for on this holy ground
You'd hear the 'twenties cry from every stone
And Bye-Bye Blackbird on the saxophone
If only History were wired for sound.

Osbert Lancaster

REMEMBER

Remember me when I am gone away,
Gone far away into the silent land;
When you can no more hold me by the hand,
Nor I half turn to go, yet turning stay.

Remember me when no more day by day
You tell me of our future that you plann'd:
Only remember me; you understand
It will be late to counsel then or pray.
Yet if you should forget me for a while
And afterwards remember, do not grieve:
For if the darkness and corruption leave
A vestige of the thoughts that once I had,
Better by far you should forget and smile
Than that you should remember and be sad.

Christina Rossetti

ROYAL JELLY

Mrs Taylor stopped knitting and looked up sharply at her husband.

"Albert," she said, "don't tell me you've been putting things into that child's milk?"

He sat there grinning.

"Well, have you or haven't you?"

"It's possible," he said.

"I don't believe it."

He had a strange, fierce way of grinning that showed his teeth.

"Albert," she said. "Stop playing with me like this."

"Yes, dear, alright."

"You haven't *really* put anything into her milk, have you? Answer me properly, Albert. This could be serious with such a tiny baby."

"The answer is yes, Mabel."

"*Albert Taylor*. How could you?"

"Now don't get over-excited," he said. "I'll tell you all about it if you really want me to, but for heaven's sake keep your hair on."

"It was beer!" she cried. "I just know it was beer!"

"Don't be so daft, Mabel, please."

"Then what was it?"

Albert laid his pipe down carefully on the table beside him and leaned back in the chair. "Tell me," he said, "did you by any chance happen to hear me mentioning something called royal jelly?"

"I did not."

"It's magic," he said. "Pure magic."

Roald Dahl

THE HORLA

13 August. When certain illnesses affect you, all the springs in your physical being seem broken, all your energy exhausted, all your muscles as soft as flesh and your flesh as liquid as water. In a strange, distressing way, I feel as if all this had happened to my spiritual being. I no longer have any strength, any courage, any control over myself, even any power to set my will in motion. I can no longer will anything; but someone wills things for me – and I obey.

14 August. I am done for! Someone is in possession of my mind and controlling it! Someone is directing my every act, my every movement, my every thought. I no longer count for anything within myself; I am nothing but a terrified, captive spectator of all the things I do. I want to go out. I cannot. He does not want to; and I remain, trembling and panic-stricken in the armchair where he keeps me seated. I want no more than to stand up, to rise from my seat so that I may believe that I am still my own master. I cannot! I am riveted to my chair, and my chair cleaves to the floor, so that no power on earth could possibly lift us.

Then, all of a sudden, I must, must, must go to the bottom of my garden to pick some strawberries and eat them. And I go. I pick some strawberries and I eat them! Oh, God! God! God! Is there a God? If there is, then deliver me! Save me! Help me! Forgive me! Take pity on me! Have mercy on me! Save me! Oh, what suffering! What torment! What terror!

Guy de Maupassant

WALK TWO MOONS

The boy came out of nowhere. Gramps saw him first and whispered, "Get behind me, chickabiddy. You too," he said to Gram. The boy was about fifteen or sixteen, with shaggy dark hair. He wore blue jeans and no shirt, and his chest was brown and muscular. In his hand he held a long bowie knife, its sheath fastened to his belt. He was standing next to Gramps' pants on the bank.

I thought of Phoebe and knew that if she were here, she would be warning us that the boy was a lunatic who would hack us all to pieces. I was wishing we had never stopped at the river, and that my grandparents would be more cautious, maybe even a little more like Phoebe who saw danger everywhere.

As the boy stared at us, Gramps said, "Howdy."

The boy said, "This here's private property."

Gramps looked all around. "Is it? I didn't see any signs."

"It's private property."

"Why, heck," Gramps said, "this here's a river. I never heard of no river being private property."

The boy picked up Gramps' pants and slid his hand into a pocket. "This land where I'm standing is private property."

Sharon Creech

RED SKY IN THE MORNING

"My brother Benedict," I said to Miranda, "is not a monster, and if I ever hear you, or anyone else in this room, using that word again, I will personally murder you with my bare hands."

There was a total, unnatural silence. The entire cloakroom, full of about thirty girls, was listening.

"But," I went on, "he is severely handicapped. He's got hydrocephalus. He'll never be like other children, but he knows how to laugh, and love people, and he's sweet, and adorable, and if you want to know why I didn't tell you before, it's because I knew you'd call him dreadful things, and laugh at him, and he's not a... not a..." and then I burst into tears.

Looking back, I suppose it was the best thing I could have done, though I felt an awful fool at the time. But I couldn't have kept up the magnificent anger etc for much longer. They all flocked round me, anyway, and I heard Miranda say,

"Honestly, I didn't mean..."

and Debbie, sounding uncharacteristically furious, saying,

"Shut up, you. You've done enough already." And then she thrust a tissue into my hand, and said,

"Poor old Pee-wit, you should have told us ages ago. We're really sorry about it. You can see that, can't you?"

And then the bell rang for the first lesson.

Elizabeth Laird

WATCHING THE WATCHER

Then he smelt the bacon. Someone was frying bacon, and for a second his teeth bit into the hot, crisp fat and he was terribly hungry. He combed his hair quickly. He could imagine it all: with fried bread and mushrooms on the plate too. He'd phone home after breakfast, absolutely definitely, though he was unwilling to keep his uncle waiting after witnessing his quick temper.

Oddly, the kitchen didn't smell of bacon. It was still and cold and actually smelt of damp dishcloths and yesterday's curry. Henry couldn't even see a kettle so he ran the tap in the sink and drank awkwardly from the stream of water. It tasted odd and sweet and curled down his chin and neck on to his shirt and made him shiver. Perhaps he had imagined the bacon, like travellers imagine oases of palm trees in the empty desert. It was not as if the Constables had big fry-ups at home and he was missing them. It was just... odd. Anyway, his appetite had gone now.

Back home they would have all finished breakfast and gone out, except his mother. She'd be there, tidying away, getting ready for Sunday lunch. If he phoned now he'd catch her alone. She'd be really pleased. He only wanted a quick word — though he told himself he didn't even want that. He went back into the hall and dialled the first three digits, then stopped. It sounded too loud, especially when he didn't know for sure where his uncle was. He carefully replaced the receiver, and looked over his shoulder. No-one was there. Only the figures in the picture held their steady gaze under the dappled forest light.

Gaye Hiçyilmaz

THE SECRET

The house was silent, blank. Even on the path you could feel the coldness coming from it, and the emptiness. Roy called to Mum and Nicky through the letter box, but they weren't there. His voice echoed flatly in the little hall, and his voice was the only sound in the deadness. He didn't cry; some things are too bad to cry about. Instead he sat on the doorstep, and pressed his back against the door. There was a tiny roof over the step, and that gave some protection against the rain but not much. And it was real after all, there was no getting away from it! The station was real, and the empty house was real, and he was really here, sitting on the doorstep in the rain. Cold and despair closed in on him from all sides. They squashed him; he felt himself shrinking. Soon he would be just a dot, sitting all alone, outside a house with nobody inside it.

And it might be quite a good thing to be just a dot – then he could get through the letter box. Or the keyhole perhaps, like Alice in Wonderland when she drank that magic stuff. Or what about that space in the window, where it didn't fit properly? If he was just a dot, he could get through that space. That space was why they had to be specially careful to keep the window locked all the time, because burglars could get in else, Mum said.

And it was a pity the window was locked, because if it wasn't *he* could get in and be a burglar, perhaps...

Ruth Thomas

NORTHERN LIGHTS

Then she ran out and on as fast as she could towards her own dormitory. The corridors were full now: children running this way and that, vivid with excitement, for the word *escape* had got around. The oldest were making for the store-rooms where the clothing was kept, and herding the younger ones with them. Adults were trying to control it all, and none of them knew what was happening. Shouting, pushing, crying, jostling people were everywhere.

Through it all Lyra and Pantalaimon darted like fish, making always for the dormitory, and just as they reached it, there was a dull explosion from behind that shook the building.

The other girls had fled: the room was empty. Lyra dragged the locker to the corner, jumped up, hauled the furs out of the ceiling, felt for the alethiometer. It was still there. She tugged the furs on quickly, pulling the hood forward, and then Pantalaimon, a sparrow at the door, called:

"Now!"

She ran out. By luck a group of children who'd already found some cold weather clothing were racing down the corridor towards the main entrance, and she joined them, sweating, her heart thumping, knowing that she had to escape or die.

Philip Pullman

THE WHEEL OF SURYA

"This was my family." His voice was harsh. "I, too, had twins. They were both girls, Anna and Rebecca, see here!"

He held out a photograph of two young girls. They had long, dark curls, and pretty round faces with mischievous eyes.

"I had a son, Felix, and a wife, and sisters and brothers, cousins, uncles – just as you did, my dear; see here, and here and here..." he held out one photograph after another with trembling hands.

"Where are they?" asked Marvinder, fearfully. Doctor Silbermann suddenly looked old and crumpled as he turned his face away to hide his tears.

"Dead, my dear. All gone. In India, Hindus, Muslims and Sikhs were killing each other; in my country, the Nazis were slaughtering Jews. You see, we both have something in common. We have both been through a holocaust."

He picked up the violin again. "You know, even your friends, the Chadwicks, endured a kind of holocaust. They lost their twins, and the grief they feel about that must be as bad as the grief I feel for my children, and you for your mother; and we all feel guilt, because we are alive and they are dead. I don't know what God will do, my dear. All I know is that we, who are alive, have to go on living, and find a way of living. I play the violin to heal my pain. It sounds as though the Chadwicks did too."

Jamila Gavin

GRADE EIGHT

MIRROR

I am silver and exact. I have no preconceptions.
Whatever I see I swallow immediately
Just as it is, unmisted by love or dislike.
I am not cruel, only truthful –
The eye of a little god, four-cornered.
Most of the time I meditate on the opposite wall.
It is pink, with speckles. I have looked at it so long
I think it is a part of my heart. But it flickers.
Faces and darkness separate us over and over.

Now I am a lake. A woman bends over me.
Searching my reaches for what she really is.
Then she turns to those liars, the candles or the moon.
I see her back, and reflect it faithfully.
She rewards me with tears and an agitation of hands.
I am important to her. She comes and goes.
Each morning it is her face that replaces the darkness.
In me she has drowned a young girl, and in me an old woman
Rises toward her day after day, like a terrible fish.

Sylvia Plath

THE TROUT

Flat on the bank I parted
Rushes to ease my hands
In the water without a ripple
And tilt them slowly downstream
To where he lay, light as a leaf,
In his fluid sensual dream.

Bodiless lord of creation
I hung briefly above him
Savouring my own absence
Senses expanding in the slow
Motion, the photographic calm
That grows before action.

As the curve of my hands
Swung under his body
He surged, with visible pleasure.
I was so preternaturally close
I could count every stipple
But still cast no shadow, until

The two palms crossed in a cage
Under the lightly pulsing gills.
Then (entering my own enlarged
Shape, which rode on the water)
I gripped. To this day I can
Taste his terror on my hands.

John Montague

ON KILLING A TREE

It takes much time to kill a tree,
Not a simple jab of the knife
Will do it. It has grown
Slowly consuming the earth,
Rising out of it, feeding
Upon its crust, absorbing
Years of sunlight, air, water,
And out of its leprous hide
Sprouting leaves.

So hack and chop
But this alone won't do it.
Not so much pain will do it.
The bleeding bark will heal
And from close to the ground
Will rise curled green twigs,
Miniature boughs
Which if unchecked will expand again
To former size.

No,
The root is to be pulled out –
Out of the anchoring earth;
It is to be roped, tied,
And pulled out – snapped out
Or pulled out entirely,
Out from the earth-cave,
And the strength of the tree exposed,
The source, white and wet,
The most sensitive, hidden
For years inside the earth.

Then the matter
Of scorching and choking
In sun and air,
Browning, hardening,
Twisting, withering,

And then it is done.

Gieve Patel

HOME-THOUGHTS, FROM ABROAD

Oh, to be in England
Now that April's there,
And whoever wakes in England
Sees, some morning, unaware,
That the lowest boughs and the brushwood sheaf
Round the elm tree bole are in tiny leaf,
While the chaffinch sings on the orchard bough
In England – now!

And after April, when May follows,
And the whitethroat builds, and all the swallows!
Hark, where my blossomed pear tree in the hedge
Leans to the field and scatters on the clover
Blossoms and dewdrops – at the bent spray's edge –
That's the wise thrush; he sings each song twice over,
Lest you should think he never could recapture
The first fine careless rapture!
And though the fields look rough with hoary dew,
All will be gay when noontide wakes anew
The buttercups, the little children's dower
– Far brighter than this gaudy melon-flower!

Robert Browning

SPARROW

He's no artist:
His taste in clothes is more
dowdy than gaudy.
And his nest – that blackbird, writing
pretty scrolls on the air with the gold nib of his beak,
would call it a slum.

To stalk solitary on lawns,
to sing solitary in midnight trees,
to glide solitary over gray Atlantics –
not for him: he'd rather
a punch-up in a gutter.

He carries what learning he has
lightly – it is, in fact, based only
on the usefulness whose result
is survival. A proletarian bird.
No scholar.

But when winter soft-shoes in
and these other birds –
ballet dancers, musicians, architects –
die in the snow
and freeze to branches,
watch him happily flying
on the O-levels and A-levels
of the air.

Norman MacCaig

TRUANT

Sing a song of sunlight
My pocket's full of sky –
Starling's egg for April
Jay's feather for July.
And here's a thorn bush three bags full
Of drift-white wool.

They call him dunce, and yet he can discern
Each mouse-brown bird,

And call its name and whistle back its call,
And spy among the fern
Delicate movement of a furred
Fugitive creature hiding from the day.
Discovered secrets magnify his play
Into a vocation.

Laughing at education
He knows where the redshank hides her nest, perceives
a red-patch tremble when a coot lays seige
To water territory.
Nothing escapes his eye:
A ladybird
Slides like a blood-drop down a spear of grass;
The sapphire sparkle of a dragonfly
Redeems a waste of weeds.
Collecting acorns, telling the beads of the year
On yew tree berries, his mind's too full for speech.

Back in the classroom he can never find
Answers to dusty questions, yet could teach,
Deeper than knowledge,
Geometry of twigs
Scratched on a sunlit wall;
History in stones,
Seasons told by the fields' calendar –
Living languages of Spring and Fall.

Phoebe Hesketh

SPIRITUAL SONG OF THE ABORIGINE

I am a child of the Dreamtime People
Part of this Land, like the gnarled gumtree
I am the river, softly singing
Chanting our songs on my way to the sea
My spirit is the dust-devils
Mirages that dance on the plain
I'm the snow, the wind and the falling rain
I'm part of the rocks and the red desert earth
Red as the blood that flows in my veins
I am eagle, crow and snake that glides
Through the rainforest that clings to the mountainside
I awakened here when the earth was new
There was emu, wombat, kangaroo
No other man of a different hue
I am this land
And this land is me
I am Australia.

Hyllus Marus

WASP NEST

Be careful not to crush
This scalloped tenement:
Who knows what secrets
Winter has failed to find
Within its paper walls?

It is the universe
Looking entirely inwards,
A hanging lantern
Whose black light wriggles
Through innumerable chambers

Where hopes still sleep
In her furry pews,
The chewed dormitory
Of a forgotten tribe
That layered its wooden pearl.

It is a basket of memories,
A museum of dead work,
The spat Babel of summer
With a marvellous language
Of common endeavour.

Note: it is the fruit
Returning to the tree,
The world becoming a clock
For sleep, a matrix of pure
Energy, a book of many lives.

John Fuller

LORD OF THE FLIES

Jack shouted.

"Make a ring!"

The circle moved in and round. Robert squealed in mock terror, then in real pain.

"Ow! Stop it! You're hurting!"

The butt end of a spear fell on his back as he blundered among them.

"Hold him!"

They got his arms and legs. Ralph, carried away by a sudden thick excitement, grabbed Eric's spear and jabbed at Robert with it.

"Kill him! Kill him!"

All at once, Robert was screaming and struggling with the strength of frenzy. Jack had him by the hair and was brandishing his knife. Behind him was Roger, fighting to get close. The chant rose ritually, as at the last moment of a dance or a hunt.

"Kill the pig! Cut his throat! Kill the pig! Bash him in!"

Ralph too was fighting to get near, to get a handful of that brown, vulnerable flesh. The desire to squeeze and hurt was over-mastering.

Jack's arm came down; the heaving circle cheered and made pig-dying noises. They then lay quiet, panting, listening to Robert's frightened snivels. He wiped his face with a dirty arm, and made an effort to retrieve his status.

"Oh, my bum!"

He rubbed his rump ruefully, Jack rolled over.

"That was a good game."

William Golding

THE GREAT GATSBY

Every Friday five crates of oranges and lemons arrived from a fruiterer in New York – every Monday these same oranges and lemons left his back door in a pyramid of pulpless halves. There was a machine in the kitchen which could extract the juice of two hundred oranges in half-an-hour if a little button was pressed two hundred times by a butler's thumb.

At least once a fortnight a corps of caterers came down with several hundred feet of canvas and enough coloured lights to make a Christmas tree of Gatsby's enormous garden. On buffet tables, garnished with glistening hors d'oeuvre, spiced baked hams crowded against salads of harlequin designs and pastry pigs and turkeys bewitched to a dark gold. In the main hall a bar with a real brass rail was set up, and stocked with gins and liquors and with cordials so long forgotten that most of his female guests were too young to know one from another.

By seven o'clock the orchestra has arrived, no thin five-piece affair, but a whole pitful of oboes and trombones and saxophones and viols and cornets and piccolos, and low and high drums. The last swimmers have come in from the beach now and are dressing upstairs; the cars from New York are parked five deep in the drive, and already the halls and salons and verandas are gaudy with primary colours, and hair bobbed in strange new ways, and shawls beyond the dreams of Castile. The bar is in full swing, and floating rounds of cocktails permeate the garden outside, until the air is alive with chatter and laughter, and casual innuendo and introductions forgotten on the spot, and enthusiastic meetings between women who never knew each other's names.

F. Scott Fitzgerald

FAR FROM THE MADDING CROWD

Bathsheba was revolving in her mind whether by a bold and desperate rush she could free herself at the risk of leaving her skirt bodily behind her. The thought was too dreadful. The dress — which she had put on to appear stately at the supper — was the head and front of her wardrobe; not another in her stock became her so well. What woman in Bathsheba's position, not naturally timid, and within call of her retainers, would have bought escape from a dashing soldier at so dear a price?

"All in good time; it will soon be done, I perceive," said her cool friend.

"This trifling provokes, and — and —"

"Not too cruel!"

"— Insults me!"

"It is done in order that I may have the pleasure of apologizing to so charming a woman, which I straightway do most humbly, madam," he said, bowing low.

Bathsheba really knew not what to say.

"I've seen a good many women in my time," continued the young man in a murmur, and more thoughtfully than hitherto, critically regarding her bent head at the same time; "but I've never seen a woman so beautiful as you. Take it or leave it — be offended or like it — I don't care."

"Who are you, then, who can so well afford to despise opinion?"

"No stranger. Sergeant Troy. I am staying in this place. — There! it is undone at last, you see. Your light fingers were more eager than mine. I wish it had been the knot of knots, which there's no untying!"

This was worse and worse. She started up, and so did he. How to decently get away from him — that was her difficulty now. She sidled off inch by inch, the lantern in her hand, till she could see the redness of his coat no longer.

"Ah, Beauty; goodbye!" he said.

She made no reply, and, reaching a distance of twenty or thirty yards, turned about, and ran indoors.

Thomas Hardy

LORD ARTHUR SAVILLE'S CRIME

As he approached Cleopatra's Needle he saw a man leaning over the parapet, and as he came nearer the man looked up, the gaslight falling full upon his face.

It was Mr Podgers, the chiromantist! No-one could mistake the fat, flabby face, the gold-rimmed spectacles, the sickly feeble smile, the sensual mouth.

Lord Arthur stopped. A brilliant idea flashed across him, and he stole softly up behind. In a moment he had seized Mr Podgers by the legs, and flung him into the Thames. There was a coarse oath, a heavy splash, and all was still. Lord Arthur looked anxiously over, but could see nothing of the chiromantist but a tall hat, pirouetting in an eddy of moonlit water. After a time it also sank, and no trace of Mr Podgers was visible. Once he thought that he caught sight of the bulky misshapen figure striking out for the staircase by the bridge, and a horrible feeling of failure came over him but it turned out to be merely a reflection, and when the moon shone out from behind a cloud it passed away. At last he seemed to have realised the decree of Destiny. He heaved a deep sigh of relief, and Sybil's name came to his lips.

"Have you dropped anything, sir?" said a voice behind him suddenly.

He turned round, and saw a policeman with a bull's-eye lantern.

"Nothing of importance, sergeant," he answered, smiling, and hailing a passing hansom, he jumped in, and told the man to drive to Belgrave Square.

Oscar Wilde

A CHILD'S CHRISTMAS IN WALES

Patient, cold and callous, our hands wrapped in socks, we waited to snowball the cats. Sleek and long as jaguars and horrible-whiskered, spitting and snarling, they would slink and sidle over the white back-garden walls, and the lynx-eyed hunters, Jim and I, fur-capped and moccasined trappers from Hudson Bay, off Mumbles Road, would hurl our deadly snowballs at the green of their eyes.

The wise cats never appeared. We were so still, Eskimo-footed arctic marksmen in the muffling silence of the eternal snows — eternal, ever since Wednesday — that we never heard Mrs Prothero's first cry from her igloo at the bottom of the garden. Or, if we heard it at all, it was, to us, like the far-off challenge of our enemy and prey, the neighbour's polar cat. But soon the voice grew louder. "Fire!" cried Mrs Prothero, and she beat the dinner gong.

And we ran down the garden, with the snowballs in our arms, toward the house; and smoke, indeed, was pouring out of the dining room, and the gong was bombilating, and Mrs Prothero was announcing ruin like a town crier in Pompeii. This was better than all the cats in Wales standing on the wall in a row. We bounded into the house, laden with snowballs, and stopped at the open door of the smoke-filled room.

Something was burning alright; perhaps it was Mr Prothero, who always slept there after midday dinner with a newspaper over his face. But he was standing in the middle of the room, saying, "A fine Christmas!" and smacking at the smoke with a slipper. "Call the fire brigade," cried Mrs Prothero as she beat the gong.

"They won't be there," said Mr Prothero, "it's Christmas."

There was no fire to be seen, only clouds of smoke and Mr Prothero standing in the middle of them, waving his slipper as though he were conducting.

"Do something," he said.

And we threw all our snowballs into the smoke —

Dylan Thomas

EMMA

She considered — resolved — and, trying to smile, began —

"You will have some news to hear, now you are come back, that will rather surprise you."

"Have I?" said he quietly, and looking at her; "of what nature?"

"Oh! the best nature in the world — a wedding."

After waiting a moment, as if to be sure she intended to say no more, he replied,

"If you mean Miss Fairfax and Frank Churchill, I have heard that already."

"How is it possible?" cried Emma, turning her glowing cheeks towards him; for while she spoke, it occurred to her that he might have called at Mrs Goddard's on his way.

"I had a few lines on parish business from Mr Weston this morning, and at the end of them he gave me a brief account of what had happened."

Emma was quite relieved, and could presently say, with a little more composure,

"*You* probably have been less surprised than any of us,

for you have had your suspicions. — I have forgotten that you once tried to give me a caution. — I wish I had attended to it — but — (with a sinking voice and a heavy sigh) I seem to have been doomed to blindness."

For a moment or two nothing was said, and she was unsuspicious of having excited any particular interest, till she found her arm drawn within his, and pressed against his heart and heard him thus saying, in a tone of great sensibility, speaking low,

"Time, my dearest Emma, time will heal the wound. — Your own excellent sense — your exertions for your father's sake — I know you will not allow yourself —." Her arm was pressed again, as he added, in a more broken and subdued accent, "The feelings of the warmest friendship — Indignation — Abominable scoundrel!" — And in a louder, steadier tone, he concluded with, "He will soon be gone. They will soon be in Yorkshire. I am sorry for her. She deserves a better fate."

Jane Austen

SOPHIE'S WORLD

She was not sure Plato was right in everything he had said about the eternal patterns, but it was a beautiful thought that all living things were imperfect copies of the eternal forms in the world of ideas. Because wasn't it true that all flowers, trees, human beings, and animals were 'imperfect'?

Everything she saw around her was so beautiful and so alive that Sophie had to rub her eyes to really believe it. But nothing she was looking at now would *last*. And yet — in a hundred years the same flowers and the same animals would be here again. Even if every single flower and every single animal should fade away and be forgotten, there would be something that 'recollected' how it all looked.

Sophie gazed out at the world. Suddenly a squirrel ran up the trunk of a pine tree. It circled the trunk a few times and disappeared into the branches.

"I've seen you before!" thought Sophie. She realised that maybe it was not the same squirrel that she had seen previously, but she had seen the same 'form'. For all she knew, Plato could have been right. Maybe she really had seen the eternal 'squirrel' before − in the world of ideas, before her soul had taken residence in a human body.

Could it be true that she had lived before? Had her soul existed before it got a body to move around in? And was it really true that she carried a little golden nugget inside her − a jewel that could not be corroded by time, a soul that would live on when her own body grew old and died?

Jostein Gaarder

METAMORPHOSIS

As Gregor Samsa awoke one morning from uneasy dreams he found himself transformed in his bed into a gigantic insect. He was lying on his hard, as it were armour-plated, back and when he lifted his head a little he could see his dome-like brown belly divided into stiff arched segments on top of which the bedquilt could hardly keep in position and was about to slide off completely. His numerous legs, which were pitifully thin compared to the rest of his bulk, waved helplessly before his eyes.

What has happened to me? he thought. It was no dream. His room, a regular human bedroom, only rather too small, lay quiet between the four familiar walls. Above the table on which a collection of cloth samples was unpacked and spread out − Samsa was a commercial traveller − hung the picture which he had recently cut out of an illustrated magazine and put into a pretty gilt frame. It showed a lady, with a fur cap on and a fur stole, sitting upright and holding out to the spectator a huge fur muff into which the whole of her forearm had vanished.

Gregor's eyes turned next to the window, and the overcast sky – one could hear raindrops beating on the window gutter – made him quite melancholy. What about sleeping a little longer and forgetting all this nonsense, he thought, but it could not be done, for he was accustomed to sleep on his right side and in his present condition he could not turn himself over. However violently he forced himself towards his right side he always rolled on to his back again. He tried it at least a hundred times, shutting his eyes to keep from seeing his struggling legs, and only desisted when he began to feel in his side a faint dull ache he had never experienced before.

O God, he thought, what an exhausting job I've picked on!

Franz Kafka

BRONZE MEDAL

"WE ARE GOING TO SEE THE RABBIT..."

We are going to see the rabbit,
We are going to see the rabbit.
Which rabbit, people say?
Which rabbit, ask the children?
Which rabbit?
The only rabbit,
The only rabbit in England,
Sitting behind a barbed-wire fence
Under the floodlights, neon lights,
Sodium lights,
Nibbling grass
On the only patch of grass
In England, in England
(Except the grass by the hoardings
Which doesn't count.)
We are going to see the rabbit
And we must be there on time.

First we shall go by escalator,
Then we shall go by underground,
And then we shall go by motorway
And then by helicopterway,
And the last ten yards we shall have to go
On foot.

And now we are going
All the way to see the rabbit,
We are nearly there,
We are longing to see it,
And so is the crowd
Which is here in thousands

With mounted policemen
And big loudspeakers
And bands and banners,
And everyone has come a long way.
But soon we shall see it
Sitting and nibbling
The blades of grass
On the only patch of grass
In — but something has gone wrong!
Why is everyone so angry,
Why is everyone jostling
And slanging and complaining?

The rabbit has gone,
Yes, the rabbit has gone.
He has actually burrowed down into the earth
And made himself a warren, under the earth,
Despite all these people.
And what shall we do?
What *can* we do?

It is all a pity, you must be disappointed,
Go home and do something else for today,
Go home again, go home for today.
For you cannot hear the rabbit, under the earth,
Remarking rather sadly to himself, by himself,
As he rests in his warren, under the earth:
"It won't be long, they are bound to come,
They are bound to come and find me, even here."

Alan Brownjohn

MYCENAE

That second, unplanned visit: call it fate
Or the unconscious, anything you like,
But with time to spare, we discovered ourselves back
At the Lion Gate, the rath of Atreus,
The founded quiet of Agamemnon's palace
Where we climbed the stone path to the *megaron*
And I read the dawn speech of the rooftop watchman
And saw the Aegean from his bastion.
Then later, downhill, at the beehive tomb
Flocks of swallows, like bats out of hell or Hades,
Crisscrossed the chamber mouth, and we felt at home
By cairn and *tholos*, cyclopic wall and dolmen.
It was omen and return, an illumined limen
We'd crossed ahead of time, foreshadowed bodies.

Seamus Heaney

BINSLEY POPLARS
Felled 1879

My aspens dear, whose airy cages quelled,
Quelled or quenched in leaves the leaping sun,
All felled, felled, are all felled;
   Of a fresh and following folded rank
         Not spared, not one
         That dandled a sandalled
      Shadow that swam or sank
On meadow and river and wind-wandering weed-winding
   bank.

O if we but knew what we do
  When we delve or hew —
 Hack and rack the growing green!
  Since country is so tender
 To touch, her being so slender,
 That, like this sleek and seeing ball
 But a prick will make no eye at all,
 Where we, even where we mean
   To mend her we end her,
  When we hew or delve:
After-comers cannot guess the beauty been.
 Ten or twelve, only ten or twelve
 Strokes of havoc unselve
  The sweet especial scene,
 Rural scene, a rural scene,
 Sweet especial rural scene.

        Gerard Manley Hopkins

I REMEMBER YOU AS YOU WERE

I remember you as you were in the last autumn.
You were the grey beret and the still heart.
In your eyes the flames of the twilight fought on.
And the leaves fell in the water of your soul.

Clasping my arms like a climbing plant
the leaves garnered your voice, that was slow and at peace.
Bonfire of awe in which my thirst was burning.
Sweet blue hyacinth twisted over my soul.

I feel your eyes travelling, and the autumn is far off:
grey beret, voice of a bird, heart like a house

towards which my deep longings migrated
and my kisses fell, happy as embers.

Sky from a ship. Field from the hills:
Your memory is made of light, of smoke, of a still pond!
Beyond your eyes, farther on, the evenings were blazing.
Dry autumn leaves revolved in your soul.

Pablo Neruda

THE MAGIC SHOW

After a feast of sausage rolls
Sandwiches of various meats,
Jewelled jellies, brimming bowls
Of chocolate ice and other treats,
We children played at Blind Man's Buff
Hide and Seek, Pin-the-tail-on-Ned,
And then — when we'd had just enough
Of party-games — we all were led
Into another room to see
The Magic Show. The wizard held
A wand of polished ebony;
His white-gloved, flickering hands compelled
The rapt attention of us all.
He conjured from astonished air
A living pigeon and a fall
Of paper snowflakes; made us stare
Bewildered as a playing-card —
Unlike a leopard — changed its spots
And disappeared. He placed some starred
And satin scarves in silver pots,
Withdrew them as plain bits of rag,

Then swallowed them before our eyes.
But soon we felt attention flag
And found delighted, first surprise
Had withered like a wintry leaf;
And, when the tricks were over, we
Applauded, yet felt some relief,
And left the party willingly.
"Goodnight," we said, "and thank you for
The lovely time we've had." Outside,
The freezing night was still. We saw
Above our heads the slow clouds stride
Across the vast, unswallowable skies;
White, graceful gestures of the moon,
The stars' intent and glittering eyes,
And, gleaming like a silver spoon,
The frosty path to lead us home.
Our breath hung blossoms on unseen
Boughs of air as we paused there,
And we forgot that we had been
Pleased briefly by that conjuror,
Could not recall his tricks, or face,
Bewitched and awed, as now we were,
By magic of the common place.

Vernon Scannell

THE WILD SWANS AT COOLE

The trees are in their autumn beauty,
The woodland paths are dry,
Under the October twilight the water
Mirrors a still sky;
Upon the brimming water among the stones
Are nine-and-fifty swans.

The nineteenth autumn has come upon me
Since I first made my count;
I saw, before I had well finished,
All suddenly mount
And scatter wheeling in great broken rings
Upon their clamorous wings.

I have looked upon those brilliant creatures,
And now my heart is sore.
All's changed since I, hearing at twilight,
The first time on this shore,
The bell-beat of their wings above my head,
Trod with a lighter tread.

Unwearied still, lover by lover,
They paddle in the cold
Companionable streams or climb the air;
Their hearts have not grown old;
Passion or conquest, wander where they will,
Attend upon them still.

But now they drift on the still water,
Mysterious, beautiful;
Among what rushes will they build,
By what lake's edge or pool
Delight men's eyes when I awake some day
To find they have flown away?

W. B. Yeats

WAITING FOR THE BARBARIANS

What are we waiting for, assembled in the forum?

> The barbarians are due here today.

Why isn't anything going on in the senate?
Why are the senators sitting there without legislating?

> Because the barbarians are coming today.
> What's the point of senators making laws now?
> Once the barbarians are here, they'll do the legislating.

Why did our emperor get up so early,
and why is he sitting enthroned at the city's main gate,
in state, wearing the crown?

> Because the barbarians are coming today
> and the emperor's waiting to receive their leader.
> He's even got a scroll to give him,
> loaded with titles, with imposing names.

Why have our two consuls and praetors come out today
wearing their embroidered, their scarlet togas?
Why have they put on bracelets with so many amethysts,
rings sparkling with magnificent emeralds?
Why are they carrying elegant canes
beautifully worked in silver and gold?

> Because the barbarians are coming today
> and things like that dazzle the barbarians.
> Why don't our distinguished orators turn up as usual
> to make their speeches, say what they have to say?

Because the barbarians are coming today
and they're bored by rhetoric and public speaking.

Why this sudden bewilderment, this confusion?
(How serious people's faces have become.)
Why are the streets and squares emptying so rapidly,
everyone going home lost in thought?

Because night has fallen and the barbarians haven't
come.
And some of our men just in from the border say
there are no barbarians any longer.

Now what's going to happen to us without barbarians?
Those people were a kind of solution.

C. P. Cavafy

CAGED BIRD

A free bird leaps
on the back of the wind
and floats downstream
till the current ends
and dips his wing
in the orange sun rays
and dares to claim the sky.

But a bird that stalks
down his narrow cage
can seldom see through
his bars of rage
his wings are clipped and
his feet are tied
so he opens his throat to sing.

The caged bird sings
with a fearful trill
of things unknown
but longed for still
and his tune is heard
on the distant hill
for the caged bird
sings of freedom.

The free bird thinks of another breeze
and the trade winds soft through the sighing trees
and the fat worms waiting on a dawn-bright lawn
and he names the sky his own.

But a caged bird stands on the grave of dreams
his shadow shouts on a nightmare scream
his wings are clipped and his feet are tied
so he opens his throat to sing.

The caged bird sings
with a fearful trill
of things unknown
but longed for still
and his tune is heard
on the distant hill
for the caged bird
sings of freedom.

Maya Angelou

ANGELA'S ASHES

Sunday nights I sit outside on the pavement under Mrs Purcell's window listening to the plays on the BBC and Radio Eireann, the Irish station. You can hear plays by O'Casey, Shaw, Ibsen and Shakespeare himself, the best of all, even if he is English. Shakespeare is like mashed potatoes, you can never get enough of him. And you can hear strange plays about Greeks plucking out their eyes because they married their mothers by mistake.

One night I'm sitting under Mrs Purcell's window listening to *Macbeth*. Her daughter, Kathleen, sticks her head out the door. Come in, Frankie. My mother says you'll catch the consumption sitting on the ground in this weather.

Ah, no, Kathleen. It's all right.

No. Come in.

They give me tea and a grand cut of bread slathered with blackberry jam. Mrs Purcell says, Do you like the Shakespeare, Frankie?

I love the Shakespeare, Mrs Purcell.

Oh, he's music, Frankie, and he has the best stories in the world. I don't know what I'd do with meself of a Sunday night if I didn't have the Shakespeare.

When the play finishes she lets me fiddle with the knob on the radio and I roam the dial for distant sounds on the shortwave band, strange whispering and hissing, the whoosh of the ocean coming and going and the Morse Code dit dit dit dot. I hear mandolins, guitars, Spanish bagpipes, the drums of Africa, boatmen wailing on the Nile. I see sailors on watch sipping mugs of hot cocoa. I see cathedrals, skyscrapers, cottages. I see Bedouins in the Sahara and the French Foreign Legion, cowboys on the American prairie. I see goats skipping along the rocky coast of Greece where the shepherds are blind because they married their mothers by mistake. I see people chatting in cafés, sipping wine, strolling on boulevards and avenues. I see night women in doorways, monks chanting vespers, and here is the great boom of Big Ben, This is the BBC Overseas Service and here is the news.

Frank McCourt

ALL THE PRETTY HORSES

She pushed the tray forward between them. Please, she said. Help yourself.

I better not. I'll have crazy dreams eatin this late.

She smiled. She unfolded a small linen napkin from off the tray.

I've always had strange dreams. But I'm afraid they are quite independent of my dining habits.

Yes mam.

They have a long life, dreams. I have dreams now which I had as a young girl. They have an odd durability for something not quite real.

Do you think they mean anything?

She looked surprised. Oh yes, she said. Dont you?

Well. I dont know. They're in your head.

She smiled again. I suppose I dont consider that to be the condemnation you do. Where did you learn to play chess?

My father taught me.

He must be a very good player.

He was about the best I ever saw.

Could you not win against him?

Sometimes. He was in the war and after he come back I got to where I could beat him but I dont think his heart was in it. He dont play at all now.

That's a pity.

Yes mam. It is.

She poured their cups again.

I lost my fingers in a shooting accident, she said. Shooting live pigeons. The right barrel burst. I was 17. Alejandra's age. There is nothing to be embarrassed about. People are curious. It's only natural. I'm going to guess that the scar on your cheek was put there by a horse.

Yes mam. It was my own fault.

She watched him, not unkindly. She smiled. Scars have the strange power to remind us that our past is real. The events that cause them can never be forgotten, can they?

No mam.

Cormac McCarthy

SILAS MARNER

He stood and listened, and gazed for a long while – there was really something on the road coming towards him then, but he caught no sign of it; and the stillness and the wide trackless snow seemed to narrow his solitude, and touched his yearning with the chill of despair. He went in again, and put his right hand on the latch of the door to close it – but he did not close it: he was arrested, as he had been already since his loss, by the invisible wand of catalepsy, and stood like a graven image, with wide but sightless eyes, holding open his door, powerless to resist either the good or evil that might enter there. When Marner's sensibility returned, he continued the action which had been arrested, and closed his door, unaware of the chasm in his consciousness, unaware of any intermediate change, except that the light had grown dim, and that he was chilled and faint. He thought he had been too long standing at the door and looking out. Turning towards the hearth, where the two logs had fallen apart, and sent forth only a red uncertain glimmer, he seated himself on his fireside chair, and was stooping to push his logs together, when, to his blurred vision, it seemed as if there were gold on the floor in front of the hearth. Gold! – his own gold – brought back to him as mysteriously as it had been taken away! He felt his heart begin to beat violently, and for a few moments he was unable to stretch out his hand and grasp the restored treasure. The heap of gold seemed to glow and get larger beneath his agitated gaze. He leaned forward at last, and stretched forth his hand; but instead of the hard coin with the familiar resisting outline, his fingers encountered soft warm curls. In utter amazement, Silas fell on his knees and bent his head low to examine the marvel: it was a sleeping child – a round, fair thing, with soft yellow rings all over its head.

George Eliot

BEHIND THE SCENES AT THE MUSEUM

Frank came home after the second battle of Ypres; he'd been in hospital in Southport with a septic foot and was given a few days' leave before going back to the Front. It was odd because before the war they'd hardly known him yet now he seemed like an old friend and when he came knocking at the back door they both hugged him and made him stay to tea. Nell ran out and got herrings and Lillian cut bread and put out jam and even Rachel asked how he was doing. But when they were all sat round the table, drinking their tea from the best service, the one that had gold rims and little blue forget-me-nots, Frank found himself unexpectedly tongue-tied. He had thought there were a lot of things about the war he wanted to tell them but was surprised to discover that the neat triangles of bread and jam and the prettiness of the little blue forget-me-nots somehow precluded him from talking about trench foot and rats, let alone the many different ways of dying he had witnessed. The smell of death clearly had no place in the parlour of Lowther Street, with the snowy cloth on the table and the glass-bead fringed lamp and the two sisters who had such soft, lovely hair that Frank ached to bury his face in it. He was thinking all these things while chewing his bread and casting around desperately for conversation, until with a nervous gulp from the gold and forget-me-nots he said, "That's a grand cup, you should taste the tea we get," and told them about the chlorinated water in the trenches. When he saw the look of horror on their faces he felt ashamed that he'd ever wanted to talk about death.

Kate Atkinson

OLD ST PAUL'S

The consternation now began. The whole city was panic-stricken; nothing was talked of but the plague – nothing planned but means of arresting its progress – one grim and ghastly idea possessed the minds of all. Like a hideous phantom stalking the streets at noon-day, and scaring all in its path, Death took his course through London, and selected his prey at pleasure. The alarm was further increased by the predictions confidently made as to the vast numbers who would be swept away by the visitation; by the prognostications of astrologers; by the prophesyings of enthusiasts; by the denunciations of preachers, and by the portents and prodigies reported to have occurred. During the long and frosty winter preceding this fatal year, a comet appeared in the heavens, the sickly colour of which was supposed to forebode the judgement about to follow. Blazing stars and other meteors, of a lurid hue and strange and preternatural shape, were likewise seen. The sun was said to have set in streams of blood, and the moon to have shone without reflecting a shadow; grisly shapes appeared at night — strange clamours and groans were heard in the air — hearses, coffins, and heaps of unburied dead were discovered in the sky, and great cakes and clots of blood were found in the Tower moat; while a marvellous double tide occurred at London Bridge. All those prodigies were currently reported, and in most cases believed.

William Harrison Ainsworth

FUGITIVE PIECES

To celebrate our first Toronto snowfall, Athos decided we should have a banquet. He sent me out into the transformed street to buy some fish. Those first months when I went out alone, I never ventured past the few stores near the flat. That day, the street looked so extraordinary I decided to walk a bit further. I entered a new grocery, shuffled my boots on the mat and waited. A man came from the back of the store and looked down at me, his large hands dangling over the counter. His apron was smeared. In a thick accent he barked, "What do you want?" I was riveted by the sound of his shouting voice. He barked again, "What did you come here for?"

"Fresh fish," I whispered.

"No! We have suspicions." He raised his voice. "We have suspicions."

I rushed out the door.

Athos was slicing mushrooms by the sink. "What kind of fish did you get? Barbounia? Glossa? I wish Daphne were here to make her kalamarakia!" I stood in the doorway. After a moment he looked up and saw my face. "Jakob, what happened?"

I told him. Athos wiped his hands, shook his slippers off

his feet, and said grimly, "Come."

I waited outside the store. I heard an uproar. Laughter. Athos came outside, grinning with relief. "It's alright, it's alright. He was saying 'chickens' not 'suspicions'." Athos began to laugh. He was standing in the street laughing, I glared at him, heat rising into my face. "I'm sorry, Jakob, I just can't help it... I haven't laughed in so long... Come in, come in..."

I would never enter that store again.

I knew I was being ridiculous, even as I pulled away from him and walked back to the flat alone.

Anne Michaels

WIVES AND DAUGHTERS

"I do like hearing of a love affair," murmured Miss Phoebe. "Then if you'll let me get on with my story, you shall hear of mine," said Mr Gibson, quite beyond his patience with their constant interruptions.

"Yours!" said Miss Phoebe, faintly.

"Bless us and save us!" said Miss Browning, with less sentiment in her tone; "what next?"

"My marriage, I hope," said Mr Gibson, choosing to take her expression of intense surprise literally. "And that's what I came to speak to you about."

A little hope darted up in Miss Phoebe's breast. She had often said to her sister, in the confidence of curling-time (ladies wore curls in those days), 'that the only man who could ever bring her to think of matrimony was Mr Gibson; but that if he ever proposed, she should feel bound to accept him, for poor dear Mary's sake'; never explaining what exact style of satisfaction she imagined she should give to her dead friend by marrying her late husband. Phoebe played nervously with the strings of her black silk apron. Like the Caliph in the Eastern story, a whole lifetime of possibilities passed through her mind in an instant, of which possibilities the question of questions was, Could she leave her sister? Attend, Phoebe, to the present moment, and listen to what is being said before you distress yourself with a perplexity which will never arise.

"Of course it has been an anxious thing for me to decide who I should ask to be the mistress of my family, the mother of my girl; but I think I've decided rightly at last. The lady I have chosen —"

"Tell us at once who she is, there's a good man," said straightforward Miss Browning.

"Mrs Kirkpatrick," said the bridegroom-elect.

Elizabeth Gaskell

HOW GREEN WAS MY VALLEY

In the Valley it was pitch black, with only a light from the farm. The moon was on us, but not yet high enough to see over the mountain. I knew well we would perish of cold if we were there much longer, so I covered Marged as far as I could, and then made a start to light a fire with twigs. In a few minutes I had a fire roaring by the rock and giving good heat, too, so I pulled Marged where she would have warmth, and started back to Gwil's for help.

Halfway down in the darkness of trees I heard her screaming again, but it only made me travel faster, and farther down by the first lot of rocks I saw Gwilym with some men carrying lanterns, all beating the briars, and some of them pushing the lamps under the hedges. I shouted until I was almost into them, but the wind was out of me, and Gwilym dropped his lantern to run and meet me when the other men shouted.

He and most of them started up the mountain ahead, with me on the shoulders of a big collier who was straight from the pit, no bath, black, and smelling of coal and strong tobacco. We were at the top almost as soon as the others, because I knew the way, and Gwil and his men came up on the wrong side of the rock, and had to run all the way round to where the fire was burning.

Up over the edge and out on the flat we ran, and across to the fire. The two men who were there first started to shout and ran into showers of sparks, beating with their caps and jumping back again. Gwil came round and stopped, staring, and then screamed, and ran to go in the flames, but the other men held him away, and they fought with him to hold him down.

More men were all round the fire trying to stamp it out and getting in my way. Then they stood clear of the heat as we came closer, and I could see.

Marged was lying in the fire, and burning, with smoke.

Richard Llewellyn

SILVER MEDAL

THE FACE OF THE HORSE

Animals do not sleep. At night
They stand over the world like a stone wall.

The cow's retreating head
Rustles the straw with its smooth horns,
The rocky brow a wedge
Between age-old cheek bones,
And the mute eyes
Turning sluggishly.

There's more intelligence and beauty in the horse's face.
He hears the talk of leaves and stones.
Intent, he knows the animal's cry
And the nightingale's murmur in the copse.

And knowing all, to whom may he recount
His wonderful visions?
The night is hushed. In the dark sky
Constellations rise.
The horse stands like a knight keeping watch,
The wind plays in his light hair,
His eyes burn like two huge worlds,
And his mane lifts like the imperial purple.

And if a man should see
The horse's magical face,
He would tear out his own impotent tongue
And give it to the horse. For
This magical creature is surely worthy of it.

Then we should hear words.
Words large as apples. Thick
As honey or buttermilk.
Words which penetrate like flame
And, once within the soul, like fire in some hut,
Illuminate its wretched trappings.
Words which do not die
And which we celebrate in song.

But now the stable is empty,
The trees have dispersed,
Pinch-faced morning has swaddled the hills,
Unlocked the fields for work.
And the horse, caged within its shafts,
Dragging a covered wagon,
Gazes out of its meek eyes,
Upon the enigmatic, stationary world.

Nikolai Alekseevich Zabolotsky

THERE WAS A CHILD ONCE

There was a child once.
He came to play in my garden;
He was quite pale and silent.
Only when he smiled I knew everything about him,
I knew what he had in his pockets,
And I knew the feel of his hands in my hands
And the most intimate tones of his voice.
I led him down each secret path,
Showing him the hiding-place of all my treasures.
I let him play with them, every one,
I put my singing thoughts in a little silver cage
And gave them to him to keep...

It was very dark in the garden
But never dark enough for us. On tiptoe we walked among
   the deepest shades;
We bathed in the shadow pools beneath the trees,
Pretending we were under the sea.
Once – near the boundary of the garden –
We heard steps passing along the World-road;
Oh, how frightened we were!
I whispered: "Have you ever walked along that road?"
He nodded, and we shook the tears from our eyes...
There was a child once.
He came – quite alone – to play in my garden;
He was pale and silent.
When we met we kissed each other,
But when he went away, we did not even wave.

Katherine Mansfield

YOU BEGIN

You begin this way:
this is your hand,
this is your eye,
that is a fish, blue and flat
on the paper, almost
the shape of an eye.
This is your mouth, this an O
or a moon, whichever
you like. This is yellow.

Outside the window
is the rain, green
because it is summer, and beyond that
the trees and then the world,

which is round and has only
the colours of these nine crayons.

This is the world, which is fuller
and more difficult to learn than I have said.
You are right to smudge it that way
with the red and then
the orange: the world burns.

Once you have learned these words
you will learn that there are more
words than you can ever learn.
The word *hand* floats above your hand
like a small cloud over a lake.
The word *hand* anchors
your hand to this table,
your hand is a warm stone
I hold between two words.

This is your hand, these are my hands, this is the world,
which is round but not flat and has more colours
than we can see.

It begins, it has an end,
this is what you will
come back to, this is your hand.

Margaret Atwood

THE CHRISTMAS TREE

Put out the lights now!
Look at the Tree, the rough tree dazzled
In oriole plumes of flame,
Tinselled with twinkling frost fire, tasselled
With stars and moons — the same
That yesterday hid in the spinney and had no fame
Till we put out the lights now.

Hard are the nights now:
The fields at moonrise turn to agate,
Shadows are cold as jet;
In dyke and furrow, in copse and faggot
The frost's tooth is set;
And stars are the sparks whirled out by the north
                                    wind's fret
On the flinty nights now.

So feast your eyes now
On mimic star and moon-cold bauble:
Worlds may wither unseen,
But the Christmas Tree is a tree of fable,
A phoenix in evergreen,
And the world cannot change or chill what its
                                    mysteries mean
To your hearts and eyes now.

The vision dies now
Candle by candle: the tree that embraced it
Returns to its own kind,
To be earthed again and weather as best it
May the frost and the wind.
Children, it too had its hour — you will not mind
If it lives or dies now.

Cecil Day Lewis

INSTRUCTIONS TO AN ACTOR

Now, boy, remember this is the great scene.
You'll stand on a pedestal behind a curtain,
the curtain will be drawn, and then you don't move
for eighty lines; don't move, don't speak, don't breathe.
I'll stun them all out there, I'll scare them,
make them weep, but it depends on you.
I warn you eighty lines is a long time,
but you don't breathe, you're dead,
you're a dead queen, a statue,
you're dead as stone, new-carved,
new-painted and the paint not dry
– we'll get some red to keep your lip shining –
and you're a mature woman, you've got dignity,
some beauty still in middle age, and
you're kind and true, but you're dead,
your husband thinks you're dead,
the audience thinks you're dead,
and you don't breathe, boy, I say
you don't even blink for eighty lines,
if you blink you're out!
Fix your eye on something and keep watching it.
Practise when you get home. It can be done.
And you move at last – music's the cue.
When you hear a mysterious solemn jangle
of instruments, make yourself ready.
Five lines more, you can lift a hand.
It may tingle a bit, but lift it –
slow, slow –
O this is where I hit them
right between the eyes, I've got them now –
I'm making the dead walk –

you move a foot, slow, steady, down,
you guard your balance in case you're stiff,
you move, you step down, down from the pedestal,
control your skirt with one hand, the other hand
you now hold out –
O this will melt their hearts if nothing does –
to your husband who wronged you long ago
and hesitates in amazement
to believe you are alive.
Finally he embraces you, and there's nothing
I can give you to say, boy,
but you must show that you have forgiven him.
Forgiveness, that's the thing. It's like a second life.
I know you can do it. – Right then, shall we try?

Edwin Morgan

IN MEMORY OF MY GRANDFATHER

Swearing about the weather he walked in
like an old tree and sat down;
his beard charred with tobacco, his voice
rough as the bark of his cracked hands.

Whenever he came it was the wrong time.
Roots spread over the hearth, tripped
whoever tried to move about the room;
the house was cramped with only furniture.

But I was glad of his coming. Only
through him could I breathe in the sun
and smell the fields. His clothes reeked
of the soil and the world outside;

geese and cows were the colour he made them,
he knew the language of birds and brought them
singing out of his beard, alive
to my blankets. He was winter and harvest.

Plums shone in his eyes when he rambled
of orchards. With giant thumbs he'd split
an apple through the core, and juice
flowed from his ripe, uncultured mouth.

Then, hearing the room clock chime,
he walked from my ceiling of farmyards
and returned to his forest of thunder;
the house regained silence and corners.

Slumped there in my summerless season
I longed for his rough hands and words
to break the restrictions of my bed,
to burst like a tree from my four walls.

But there was no chance again of miming
his habits or language. Only now,
years later in a cramped city, can I
be grateful for his influence and love.

Edward Storey

A CERTAIN LADY

Oh, I can smile for you, and tilt my head,
    And drink your rushing words with eager lips,
And paint my mouth for you a fragrant red,
    And trace your brows with tutored fingertips.
When you rehearse your list of loves to me,
    Oh, I can laugh and marvel, rapturous-eyed.

And you laugh back, nor can you ever see
 The thousand little deaths my heart has died.
And you believe, so well I know my part,
 That I am gay as morning, light as snow,
And all the straining things within my heart
 You'll never know.

Oh, I can laugh and listen, when we meet,
 And you bring tales of fresh adventurings, —
Of ladies delicately indiscreet,
 Of lingering hands, and gently whispered things.
And you are pleased with me, and strive anew
 To sing me sagas of your late delights.
Thus do you want me — marveling, gay, and true,
 Nor do you see my staring eyes of nights.
And when, in search of novelty, you stray,
 Oh, I can kiss you blithely as you go...
And what goes on, my love, while you're away,
 You'll never know.

Dorothy Parker

MY RIVAL'S HOUSE

is peopled with many surfaces.
Ormolu and gilt, slipper satin,
lush velvet couches,
cushions so stiff you can't sink in.
Tables polished clear enough to see distortions in.

We take our shoes off at her door,
shuffle stocking-soled, tiptoe — the parquet floor
is beautiful and its surface must
be protected. Dust
cover, drawn shade,
won't let the surface colour fade.

Silver sugar-tongs and silver salver,
my rival serves us tea.
She glosses over him and me.
I am all edges, a surface, a shell
and yet my rival thinks she means me well.
But what squirms beneath her surface I can tell.
Soon, my rival
capped tooth, polished nail
will fight, fight foul for her survival.
Deferential, daughterly, I sip
and thank her nicely for each bitter cup.

And I have much to thank her for.
This son she bore —
first blood to her —
never, never can escape scot free
the sour potluck of family.
And oh how close
this family that furnishes my rival's place.

Lady of the house.
Queen bee.
She is far more unconscious,
far more dangerous than me.
Listen, I was always my own worst enemy.
She has taken even this from me.

She dishes up her dreams for breakfast.
Dinner, and her salt tears pepper our soup.
She won't
give up.

Liz Lochhead

THE LADY OF THE CAMELLIAS

A great white shroud covered the corpse, closely outlining some of its contours. This shroud was almost completely eaten away at one end, and left one of the feet visible.

I was nearly fainting, and at the moment of writing these lines I see the whole scene over again in all its imposing reality.

"Quick," said the inspector. Thereupon one of the men put out his hand, began to unscrew the shroud, and taking hold of it by one end suddenly laid bare the face of Marguerite.

It was terrible to see, it is horrible to relate. The eyes were nothing but two holes, the lips had disappeared, vanished, and the white teeth were tightly set. The black hair, long and dry, was pressed tightly about the forehead, and half veiled the green hollows of the cheeks; and yet I recognised in this face the joyous white and rose face that I had seen so often.

Armand, unable to turn away his eyes, had put the handkerchief to his mouth and bit it.

For my part, it was as if a circle of iron tightened about my head, a veil covered my eyes, a rumbling filled my ears, and all I could do was to unstop a smelling bottle which I happened to have with me, and to draw in long breaths of it.

Through this bewilderment I heard the inspector say to Duval, "Do you identify?"

"Yes," replied the young man in a dull voice.

"Then fasten it up and take it away," said the inspector.

The gravediggers put back the shroud over the face of the corpse, fastened up the coffin, took hold of each end of it, and began to carry it toward the place where they had been told to take it.

Armand did not move. His eyes were fixed upon the empty grave; he was as white as the corpse which he had just seen. He looked as if he had been turned to stone.

Alexander Dumas

JILL

It was curious that he felt no hesitancy about what to write. True, he made several drafts, but that was because he found it hard to imitate his sister's hand from the single addressed envelope. It was cramped, like his own, and might suggest immaturity if subtly coarsened. He worked intently, like an etcher or forger, his feet locked together and his hair shining in the electric light. Christopher was lounging in bed in the other room.

When he had finished he wiped his hands on his trousers and grinned.

> *Willow Gables School,*
> *Nr Mallerton,*
> *Derbyshire.*

Dear John,

You said you would write to me, but of course you haven't, you never do. So I am writing to you instead, so mind you answer.

How are you getting on? Tell me everything about your college and the rooms you have; what work you're doing (remember the bet we made); who your tutor is, do I know him and what's he like? I long to Know All. Give me plenty of details because Maisie Fenton's got a brother at Cambridge and is being just insufferable about him. Still, you don't know Maisie Fenton. (Lucky you!)

I really haven't any news for you; this place is as usual — need I say more? I came top in English this fortnight (pom-tiddly-om-pom) and intend to do so for the rest of the term for reasons which are Secret.

When do your holidays start? Before ours, I expect — for a change!

> *Much love,*
> *Jill.*

P.S. – We're going to some incredible concert thing in Manchester, so I shall post this there if poss. I really don't trust the school box anymore after what happened last term...
P.P.S. – It's raining. No hockey!

He had just finished copying the last draft when he heard Christopher getting up, so, carelessly stuffing it into the original envelope, he put it onto the mantelpiece and strolled out.

Philip Larkin

GREAT EXPECTATIONS

So she sat, corpse-like, as we played at cards; the frillings and trimmings on her bridal dress looking like earthy paper. I knew nothing then of the discoveries that are occasionally made of bodies buried in ancient times, which fall to powder in the moment of being distinctly seen; but I have often thought since, that she must have looked as if the admission of the natural light of day would have struck her to dust.

"He calls the knaves, Jacks, this boy!" said Estella with disdain, before our first game was out. "And what coarse hands he has. And what thick boots!"

I had never thought of being ashamed of my hands before; but I began to consider them a very indifferent pair. Her contempt was so strong, that it became infectious, and I caught it.

She won the game, and I dealt. I misdealt, as was only natural, when I knew she was lying in wait for me to do wrong; and she denounced me for a stupid, clumsy labouring-boy.

"You say nothing of her," remarked Miss Havisham to me, as she looked on. "She says many hard things of you, but you say nothing of her. What do you think of her?"

"I don't like to say," I stammered.

"Tell me in my ear," said Miss Havisham, bending down.

"I think she is very proud," I replied in a whisper.

"Anything else?"

"I think she is very pretty."

"Anything else?"

"I think she is very insulting." (She was looking at me then, with a look of supreme aversion.)

"Anything else?"

"I think I should like to go home."

"And never see her again, though she is so pretty?"

"I am not sure that I shouldn't like to see her again, but I should like to go home now."

Charles Dickens

THE GOD OF SMALL THINGS

Estha waited until Rahel got in, then took his place, sitting astride the little boat as though it were a seesaw. He used his legs to push the boat away from the shore. As they lurched into the deeper water they began to row diagonally upstream, against the current, the way Velutha had taught them to. ("If you want to end up there, you must aim *there*.")

In the dark they couldn't see that they were in the wrong lane on a silent highway full of muffled traffic. That branches, logs, parts of trees, were motoring towards them at some speed.

They were past the Really Deep, only yards from the Other Side, when they collided with a floating log and the little boat tipped over. It had happened to them often enough on previous expeditions across the river, and they would swim after the boat and, using it as a float, dog-paddle to the shore. This time, they couldn't see their boat in the dark. It was swept away in the current. They headed for the shore, surprised at how much effort it took them to cover that short distance.

Estha managed to grab a low branch that arched down into the water. He peered downriver through the darkness to see if he could see the boat at all.

"I can't see anything. It's gone."

Rahel, covered in slush, clambered ashore and held a hand out to help Estha pull himself out of the water. It took them a few minutes to catch their breath and register the loss of the boat. To mourn its passing.

"And all our food is spoiled," Rahel said to Sophie Mol and was met with silence. A rushing, rolling, fishswimming silence.

"Sophie Mol?" she whispered to the rushing river. "We're here! Here! Near the Illimba tree!"

Nothing.

On Rahel's heart Pappachi's moth snapped open its sombre wings.

Out.

In.

And lifted its legs.

Up.

Down.

They ran along the bank calling out to her. But she was gone.

Arundhati Roy

THE LAST SEPTEMBER

"Now that alone," exclaimed Lady Naylor, waving her gloves in a rapid gesticulation, "would make a marriage quite fatal... Mr Lesworth, I don't want to have to imagine you miserable. I have no sons of my own, you know, and Laurence being so intellectual − And there is another thing..." She paused, and with unusual nervousness, with a movement almost of Francie's, touched her boa, her jabot, two carnations pinned in the lace. She had now to tilt straight at indecency. There was this question of money – a subject the English made free with, as free with as what was below their diaphragms, but from which her whole modesty shrank. "You may think me dreadful," she said, "but there are things in life one must face. After all, I am Lois' aunt..."

Gerald, blushing, stood agonised to attention.

"There is money," she brought out at last. "I mean, you haven't any, have you? Of course, I don't see why you should have. But two people must live, though it's all rather sordid. However, this need not arise. But I just want to show you –"

"I know she's got a beautiful home," he said glumly.

"However...You see, it's impossible every way. But first and last, she does not love you."

He was forced into the position which he would have described to a friend as bloody, of asserting she *did*. "Though I cannot think why."

"Oh, but so many girls would!" she cried earnestly. "But for Lois I do think – we all think – a school of art. She cares for her drawing intensely."

"She never speaks of it."

"Ah, that just shows... Lack of sympathy!" said the aunt with mournful complacency. "And it isn't simply your age; it would be the same thing if you were a captain or even a major. Now I do think you ought to be sensible. It can all pass off so quietly. Nobody knows except me. Now what I suggest –"

"– She might have told me she'd told you!" He stared round the changed room bitterly.

"That was just what I didn't encourage, to tell you the truth. Oh, the child was most honest. But I thought you and I should approach this quite fresh and unprejudiced."

"Did we have to?"

"Oh, Mr Lesworth!" she cried, disconcerted. She resumed, firmly but with inspiration, something between a hospital nurse and a prophetess: "The less talk, the less indirect discussion round and about things, the better, I always think."

Elizabeth Bowen

PADDY CLARKE HA HA HA

She didn't get up one morning. Da was going down to Mrs McEvoy to get her to take the babies for the day. Me and Sinbad still had to go to school.

– Get your breakfasts here, he said.

He unlocked the back door.

– Are you washed yet?

He'd gone before I could tell him that I always washed myself before I had my breakfast. I always made my own cornflakes, got the bowl and put in the flakes – never spilt them – put in the milk. Then the sugar. I used to flick my fingernail under the spoon so the sugar would be sprinkled evenly all over. But I didn't know what to do this morning; I was all mixed up. There was no bowl. I knew where she kept them. I put them away sometimes. There was no milk. It was probably still on the front step. There was only the sugar. I went over to it. I didn't want to think. I didn't want to think about my ma up in their bedroom. About her sick. I didn't want to see her. I was afraid.

Sinbad followed me.

If she wasn't sick, if she was just up in the bed, I'd have to know why she hadn't got up. I didn't want to know. I couldn't go up there. I didn't want to know. It would be back to normal when we came home from school later.

I had a spoon of sugar. I didn't keep it long enough in my mouth for it to become nice. I wasn't hungry. I wouldn't bother having any breakfast. I'd make toast. I liked the gas.

— What's wrong with Mam?

I didn't want to know.

— Shut up.

— What's wrong with her?

— Shut up.

— Is she sick?

— She's sick of you; shut up.

— Is she not well?

I liked the hiss the gas made and the smell for a little bit. I grabbed Sinbad. I made his face go close to the gas. He pushed back. He wasn't as easy to control as he used to be. His arms were strong. He couldn't beat me though. He'd never be able to do that. I'd always be bigger than him. He got away.

— I'm telling.

— Who?

— Da.

— What're you goin' to tell him? I said, moving towards him.

— You were messin' with the gas, he said.

— So what?

— We're not allowed.

He ran into the hall.

— You'll wake Ma, I said. — Then she'll never get better and you'll be to blame.

He wouldn't tell anything.

Roddy Doyle

LUCIA IN LONDON

Lucia was specially enthusiastic over a picture of Waterloo Bridge, but she had mistaken the number in the catalogue, and it proved to be a portrait of the artist's wife. Luckily she had not actually read out to Sophy that it was Waterloo Bridge, though she had said something about the river, but this was easily covered up in appreciation.

"Too wonderful," she said. "How they get to the very soul of things! What is it that Wordsworth says? 'The very pulse of the machine.' Pulsating, is it not?"

Mrs Alingsby was tall and weird and intense, dressed rather like a bird of paradise that had been out in a high gale, but very well connected. She had long straight hair which fell over her forehead, and sometimes got in her eyes, and she wore on her head a scarlet jockey-cap with an immense cameo in front of it. She hated all art that was earlier than 1923, and a considerable lot of what was later. In music, on the other hand, she was primitive, and thought Bach decadent: in literature her taste was for stories without a story, and poems without metre or meaning. But she had collected round her a group of interesting outlaws, of whom the men looked like women, and the women like nothing at all, and though nobody ever knew what they were talking about, they themselves were talked about. Lucia had been to a party of hers, where they all sat in a room with black walls, and listened to early Italian music on a spinet while a charcoal brazier on a blue hearth was fed with incense... Lucia's general opinion of her was that she might be useful up to a point, for she certainly excited interest.

"Wordsworth?" she asked. "Oh yes, I remember who you mean. About the Westmorland lakes. Such a killjoy."

She put on her large horn spectacles to look at the picture of the artist's wife, and her body began to sway with a lithe circular motion.

"Marvellous! What a rhythm!" she said. "Sigismund is the most rhythmical of them all. You ought to be painted by him. He would make something wonderful of you. Something *andante*, *adagio* almost. He's coming to see me on Sunday. Come and meet him. Breakfast about half-past twelve. Vegetarian with cocktails."

E. F. Benson

LADY'S MAID

Attending her mistress that night, Wilson found her exhausted, barely able to lift her arms so that her dress could be pulled off and her chemise slipped on. She said again and again that she was tired, oh so tired, and that she wished she could sleep a hundred years. Wilson, seeking to cheer her up, was bold enough to ask if she would like Prince Charming to wake her up at the end of her century of sleep but Miss Elizabeth shook her head and said she had no thoughts of Princes.

"Do you, Wilson?"

"Miss?"

"Do you have thoughts of Prince Charming?"

"Oh, Princes are not for the likes of me, miss."

"But you can dream, Wilson, anyone can dream, he does not have to be a Prince, exactly. Now come, do you not dream?"

Seeing her mistress more animated, Wilson knew she must humour her and respond and so she said, "Oh yes, miss, I dream, but not of Princes. I dream more of children, ma'am, to be serious, and a home."

Miss Elizabeth was quiet and Wilson worried that she had gone too far but in a moment her mistress, much calmer and more serene now, said, "That is a better dream, Wilson. But there ought to be a father for those babies you dream of, ought there not?"

"Yes, miss, but I don't seem to see him."

"Have you tried, tried hard?"

"Sometimes, miss. On Hallowe'en. Where I come from, in the North, ma'am, we have games, they are just silly games, we peel an apple and throw the peel over our shoulder and it is said to fall in the shape of a letter, the first letter of your future husband's name. And if it is done in front of a mirror and there is only a candle in the far corner of the room then it is said he will come and look over your shoulder at you if you call his name right." Wilson was startled to have her wrist gripped firmly.

"Does it work, Wilson? Have you done this? Did you see anything?"

Wilson hesitated. Was it wise to continue? But Miss Elizabeth's eyes shone and she sat up straight with excitement.

"Not exactly, miss, but once I saw a shadow and felt a presence but when I turned there was no-one there."

"Do you believe in ghosts, Wilson?"

Again, Wilson hesitated. She had not meant to start this kind of conversation. But before she could reply Miss Elizabeth had said, "For I do, Wilson, I believe in a spirit world, I *feel* it, often, there *is* something there, some actual life beyond the grave. Of that I have no doubt."

Margaret Forster

GOLD MEDAL

"I WILL LIVE AND SURVIVE"

I will live and survive and be asked:
How they slammed my head against a trestle,
How I had to freeze at nights,
How my hair started to turn grey...
But I'll smile. And will crack some joke
And brush away the encroaching shadow.
And I will render homage to the dry September
That became my second birth.
And I'll be asked: "Doesn't it hurt you to remember?"
Not being deceived by my outward flippancy.
But the former names will detonate my memory −
Magnificent as old cannon.
And I will tell of the best people in all earth,
The most tender, but also the most invincible,
How they said farewell, how they went to be tortured,
How they waited for letters from their loved ones.
And I'll be asked: what helped us to live
When there were neither letters nor any news − only walls,
And the cold of the cell, and the blather of official lies,
And the sickening promises made in exchange for betrayal.
And I will tell of the first beauty
I saw in captivity.
A frost-covered window! No spyholes, nor walls,
Nor cell-bars, nor the long-endured pain −
Only a blue radiance on a tiny pane of glass,
A cast pattern − none more beautiful could be dreamt!
The more clearly you looked, the more powerfully blossomed
Those brigand forests, campfires and birds!
And how many times there was bitter cold weather
And how many windows sparkled after that one −
But never was it repeated,

That upheaval of rainbow ice!
And anyway, what good would it be to me now,
And what would be the pretext for that festival?
Such a gift can only be received once,
And perhaps is only needed once.

Irina Ratushinskaya

THE CONDUCTOR

I am the conductor. I preside
Over the players, clothed in the swagger
Of my office. My imperative hands
Ordain volume and tempo. I am
The music's master.

This is the music, propped open before me:
Immense Unfinished Symphony of life,
Its intervals, blunt naturals and fugues,
Its resolutions, syncopations, shakes,
Scored for my players.

These are the players. (Stand up, friends,
And make your bows.) A random lot,
Amateurs all, for nothing at all disbars,
And finally all find parts that fit them
For my orchestra.

Listen! an excerpt: today's programme.
First subject, in flute's paediatric whine,
Transposed now to the key of senility,
Dribbling urine and spittle, difficult heartbeats
Plucking like harpstrings.

Each virtuoso has his own variation:
Depression's largo, schizophrenia's scherzo.
Mute music of the withdrawn, epileptic cadenzas,
The plagal cadence of the stretcher-borne dying,
Drum taps of the blind.

Listen again. The second subject
Is harder to hear, is sensed at last
In pauses, breves, a *did-not-come*, a rest,
A silence. For this symphony's name
Is also Farewell,

And as each player reaches his part's end
He tucks his instrument decently under his arm,
Snuffs out his candle, tiptoes demurely away
Into the dark and the stillness. For him
The concert's over.

I, the receptionist, must also play
My part, and go. I shoot my cuffs,
And watch my hectoring fingers, like the rest,
Sprout into rattlebones. And see
A new conductor,

Young, fetching, shifty, immortal,
Hermes bringer of dreams, the light-fingered,
Hermes who leads men's souls in another direction
From our world of unholy living
And wholly dying.

                                        U. A. Fanthorpe

THE BEGINNING

"Where have I come from, where did you pick me up?"
the baby asked its mother.

She answered half-crying, half-laughing, and clasping
the baby to her breast, —

"You were hidden in my heart as its desire, my darling.

You were in the dolls of my childhood's games; and
when with clay I made the image of my god every morning,
I made and unmade you then.

You were enshrined with our household deity, in his
worship I worshipped you.

In all my hopes and my loves, in my life in the life of
my mother you have lived.

In the lap of the deathless Spirit who rules our home
you have been nursed for ages.

When in girlhood my heart was opening its petals, you
hovered as a fragrance about it.

Your tender softness bloomed in my youthful limbs, like
a glow in the sky before the sunrise.

Heaven's first darling, twin-born with the morning light,
you have floated down the stream of the world's life, and
at last you have stranded on my heart.

As I gaze on your face, mystery overwhelms me; you
who belong to all have become mine.

For fear of losing you I hold you tight to my breast.
What magic has snared the world's treasure in these slender
arms of mine?"

Rabindranath Tagore

TWO LOOK AT TWO

Love and forgetting might have carried them
A little further up the mountainside
With night so near, but not much further up.
They must have halted soon in any case
With thoughts of the path back, how rough it was
With rock and washout, and unsafe in darkness;
When they were halted by a tumbled wall
With barbed-wire binding. They stood facing this,
Spending what onward impulse they still had
In one last look the way they must not go,
On up the failing path, where, if a stone
Or earthslide moved at night, it moved itself;
No footstep moved it. "This is all," they sighed,
"Goodnight to woods." But not so; there was more.
A doe from round a spruce stood looking at them
Across the wall, as near the wall as they.
She saw them in their field, they her in hers.
The difficulty of seeing what stood still,
Like some up-ended boulder split in two,
Was in her clouded eyes: they saw no fear there.
She seemed to think that, two thus, they were safe.
Then, as if they were something that, though strange,
She could not trouble her mind with too long,
She sighed and passed unscared along the wall.
"*This*, then, is all. What more is there to ask?"
But no, not yet. A snort to bid them wait.
A buck from round the spruce stood looking at them
Across the wall, as near the wall as they.
This was an antlered buck of lusty nostril,
Not the same doe come back into her place.
He viewed them quizzically with jerks of head,

As if to ask, "Why don't you make some motion?
Or give some sign of life? Because you can't.
I doubt if you're as living as you look."
Thus till he had them almost feeling dared
To stretch a proffering hand – and a spell-breaking.
Then he too passed unscared along the wall.
Two had seen two, whichever side you spoke from.
"This *must* be all." It was all. Still they stood,
A great wave from it going over them,
As if the earth in one unlooked-for favour
Had made them certain earth returned their love.

Robert Frost

ODE ON MELANCHOLY

No, no! go not to Lethe, neither twist
    Wolf's-bane, tight-rooted, for its poisonous wine;
Nor suffer thy pale forehead to be kist
    By nightshade, ruby grape of Proserpine;
Make not your rosary of yew-berries,
    Nor let the beetle, nor the death-moth be
      Your mournful Psyche, nor the downy owl
A partner in your sorrow's mysteries;
    For shade to shade will come too drowsily,
      And drown the wakeful anguish of the soul.

But when the melancholy fit shall fall
    Sudden from heaven like a weeping cloud,
That fosters the droop-headed flowers all,
    And hides the green hill in an April shroud;
Then glut thy sorrow on a morning rose,
    Or on the rainbow of the salt sand-wave,
      Or on the wealth of globèd peonies;

Or if thy mistress some rich anger shows,
    Emprison her soft hand, and let her rave,
        And feed deep, deep upon her peerless eyes.

She dwells with Beauty – Beauty that must die;
    And Joy, whose hand is ever at his lips
Bidding adieu; and aching Pleasure nigh,
    Turning to poison while the bee-mouth sips:
Ay, in the very temple of Delight
    Veil'd Melancholy has her sovran shrine,
        Though seen of none save him whose strenuous tongue
Can burst Joy's grape against his palate fine;
    His soul shall taste the sadness of her might,
        And be among her cloudy trophies hung.

John Keats

THE BIG HOUSE

I was only the girl under the stairs
But I was the first to notice something was wrong.
I was always first up and about, of course.
Those hens would never lay two days running
In the same place. I would rise early
And try round the haggard for fresh nests.
The mistress let me keep the egg-money.

And that particular night there were guests,
Mrs de Groot from the bridge set
And a young man who wrote stories for children,
So I wanted everything to be just right
When they trooped down to breakfast that morning.

I slept at the very top of that rambling house,
A tiny room with only a skylight window.
I had brushed my hair and straightened my dress

And was just stepping into the corridor
When it struck me. That old boarded-up door
Was flung open. A pile of rubble and half-bricks
Was strewn across the landing floor.

I went on down. I was stooping among the haystacks
When there came a clatter of hooves in the yard.
The squire's sure-footed little piebald mare
Had found her own way home, as always.
He swayed some. Then fell headlong on the cobbles.

There was not so much as a smell of whiskey on him.
People still hold he had died of fright,
That the house was haunted by an elder brother
Who was murdered for his birthright.
People will always put two and two together.
What I remember most of that particular morning
Was how calmly everyone took the thing.
The mistress insisted that life would go on quietly
As it always had done. Breakfast was served
At nine exactly. I can still hear Mrs de Groot
Telling how she had once bid seven hearts.
The young man's stories were for grown-ups, really.

Paul Muldoon

THE LETTER

If I remember right, his first letter.
Found where? My side-plate perhaps,
Or propped on our heavy brown teapot.
One thing is clear — my brother leaning
across asking *Who is he?* half-angry
as always that summer before enlistment.

Then alone in the sunlit yard, mother
unlocking a door to call *Up so early?*
– waving her yellow duster goodbye
in a small sinking cloud. The gate creaks
shut and there in the lane I am running
uphill, vanishing where the woodland starts.

The Ashground. A solid contour swept
through ripening wheat, and a fringe
of stippled green shading the furrow.
Now I am hardly breathing, gripping
the thin paper and reading *Write to me.*
Write to me please. I miss you. My angel.

Almost shocked, but repeating him line
by line, and watching the words jitter
under the pale spidery shadows of leaves.
How else did I leave the plane unheard
so long? But suddenly there it was –
a Messerschmitt low at the wood's edge.

What I see today is the window open,
the pilot's unguarded face somehow
closer than possible. Goggles pushed up,
a stripe of ginger moustache, and his eyes
fixed on my own while I stand
with the letter held out, my frock blowing,

before I am lost in cover again,
heading for home. He must have banked
at once, climbing steeply until his jump
and watching our simple village below –
the Downs swelling and flattening, speckled
with farms and bushy chalk-pits. By lunch

they found where he lay, the parachute
tight in its pack, and both hands spread
as if they could break the fall. I still
imagine him there exactly. His face pressed
close to the sweet-smelling grass. His legs
splayed wide in a candid unshamable V.

Andrew Motion

THE PARROT

The old professor of Zoology
Shook his long beard and spake these words to me:
"Compare the Parrot with the Dove. They are
In shape the same: in hue dissimilar.
The Indian bird, which may be sometimes seen
In red or black, is generally green.
His beak is very hard: it has been known
To crack thick nuts and penetrate a stone.
Alas that when you teach him how to speak
You find his head is harder than his beak.

The passionless Malay can safely drub
The pates of parrots with an iron club:
The ingenious fowls, like boys they beat at school,
Soon learn to recognise a Despot's rule.
    Now if you'd train a parrot, catch him young
While soft the mouth and tractable the tongue.
Old birds are fools: they dodder in their speech,
More eager to forget than you to teach;
They swear one curse, then gaze at you askance,
And all oblivion thickens in their glance.

Thrice blest whose parrot of his own accord
Invents new phrases to delight his Lord,
Who spurns the dull quotidian task and tries
Selected words that prove him good and wise.
Ah, once it was my privilege to know
A bird like this...
    But that was long ago!"

James Elroy Flecker

THE MAGIC LANTERN

The curtain went up on a dreadful set of the nineteenth-century Grabow era. The young girl was played by one of the famous *Sociétaires* who was well past pensionable age. She acted with brittle intensity, her wig brutally yellow, accentuating her sharp nose and painted little old woman's face. They all declaimed at walking pace or at a gallop, the heroine throwing herself down on the boards at the very bright footlights. A thirty-five-man orchestra played the vigorous sensual music without exerting themselves, skipping repeats, people went in and out of the orchestra pit, talking unconcernedly, and the oboist drank a glass of wine. The heroine screamed in heart-rending tones and yet again fell to the floor.

A strange sound then welled up from the darkness of the auditorium. I looked round and discovered to my astonishment that everyone was crying, some rather discreetly into their handkerchiefs, others openly and with pleasure. Monsieur Lebrun at my side, with his well-brushed and parted hair and well-groomed moustache, was shaking as if with fever, and out of his round black eyes clear tears were running down his well-shaven rosy cheeks, his little fat hands moving helplessly over the sharp creases of his trousers.

The curtain fell to resounding applause. The ageing girl came up front stage, her wig crooked, placed a small hand on her bony chest and stood quite still, regarding her audience with a dark unfathomable gaze. She was still in a trance, then allowed herself to be woken slowly by the jubilant cries of the faithful, all those people who had lived a life with *L'Arlésienne*, all those people who again and again had gone on a pilgrimage to a Sunday performance at the theatre, first with grandmother holding their hands and now with their own grandchildren, secure in the fact that Madame Guerlaine, eternally on the same stage, at a definite time, year after year, would throw herself down headlong by the footlights, lamenting her grief over the cruelty of life.

Everyone was shouting. The little old woman up there on the mercilessly illuminated stage had once again touched the hearts of the faithful. *Theatre as a miracle.*

Ingmar Bergman

WRITING HOME

Miss S's daily emergence from the van was highly dramatic. Suddenly and without warning the rear door would be flung open to reveal the tattered draperies that masked the terrible interior. There was a pause, then through the veils would be hurled several bulging plastic sacks. Another pause, before slowly and with great caution one sturdy slippered leg came feeling for the floor before the other followed and one had the first sight of the day's wardrobe. Hats were always a feature: a black railwayman's hat with a long neb worn slightly on the skew so that she looked like a drunken signalman or a French guardsman of the 1880s; there was her Charlie Brown pitcher's hat; and in June 1977 an octagonal straw table-mat, tied on with a chiffon scarf and a bit of cardboard for the peak. She also went in for green eyeshades. Her skirts had a telescopic appearance, as they had often been lengthened many times over by the simple expedient of sewing a strip of extra cloth around the hem, though with no attempt at matching. One skirt was made by sewing several orange dusters together. When she fell foul of authority she put it down to her clothes. Once, late at night, the police rang me from Tunbridge Wells. They had picked her up on the station, thinking her dress was a nightie. She

was indignant. "Does it look like a nightie? You see lots of
people wearing dresses like this. I don't think this style can
have got to Tunbridge Wells yet."

Miss S seldom wore stockings, and alternated between
black pumps and brown carpet slippers. Her hands and feet
were large, and she was what my grandmother would have
called "a big-boned woman". She was middle-class and spoke
in a middle-class way, though her querulous and often
resentful demeanour tended to obscure this; it wasn't a gentle
or a genteel voice. Running through her vocabulary was a
streak of schoolgirl slang. She wouldn't say she was tired,
she was "all done up"; petrol was "juice"; and if she wasn't
keen on doing something she'd say "I'm darned if I will."
All her conversation was impregnated with the vocabulary
of her peculiar brand of Catholic fanaticism ("the dire
importance of justice deeds"). It was the language of the
leaflets she wrote, the "possibly" with which she ended so
many of her sentences an echo of the "Subject to the Roman
Catholic Church in her rights etc." with which she headed
every leaflet.

Alan Bennett

OUR MAN IN HAVANA

When the Chief had guests he dined at home and cooked
his own dinner, for no restaurant satisfied his meticulous and
romantic standard. There was a story that once when he was
ill he refused to cancel an invitation to an old friend, but
cooked the meal from his bed by telephone. With a watch
before him on the bed-table he would interrupt the
conversation at the correct interval, to give directions to his
valet. "Hallo, hallo, Brewer, hallo, you should take that
chicken out now and baste it again."

It was also said that once when he had been kept late at the office he had tried to cook the meal from there, dinner had been ruined because from force of habit he had used his red telephone, the scrambler, and only strange noises resembling rapid Japanese had reached the valet's ears. The meal which he served to the Permanent Under-Secretary was simple and excellent: a roast with a touch of garlic. A Wensleydale cheese stood on the sideboard and the quiet of Albany lay deeply around them like snow. After his exertions in the kitchen the Chief himself smelt faintly of gravy.

"It's really excellent. Excellent."

"An old Norfolk recipe. Granny Brown's Ipswich Roast."

"And the meat itself… it really melts…"

"I've trained Brewer to do the marketing, but he'll never make a cook. He needs constant supervision."

They ate for a while reverently in silence; the clink of a woman's shoes along the Rope Walk was the only distraction.

"A good wine," the Permanent Under-Secretary said at last.

"'Fifty-five is coming along nicely. Still a little young?"

"Hardly."

With the cheese the Chief spoke again. "The Russian note – what does the F.O. think?"

"We are a little puzzled by the reference to the Caribbean bases." There was a crackling of Romary biscuits. "They can hardly refer to the Bahamas. They are worth about what the Yankees paid us, a few old destroyers. Yet we've always assumed that those constructions in Cuba had a Communist origin. You don't think they could have an American origin after all?"

"Wouldn't we have been informed?"

"Not necessarily, I'm afraid. Since the Fuchs case. They say we keep a good deal under our own hat too. What does your man in Havana say?"

"I'll ask him for a full assessment. How's the Wensleydale?"

"Perfect."

"Help yourself to the port."

"Cockburn'35, isn't it?"

"'Twenty-seven.'"

Graham Greene

THÉRÈSE RAQUIN

Laurent stood up and seized Camille around his waist. The clerk burst out laughing.

"No, stop it, you're tickling me!" he said. "Now that's enough larking about! Come on, stop it or you'll make me fall in!"

Laurent squeezed harder and gave a heave. Camille turned round and saw the terrifying, contorted expression on his friend's face. He did not understand, but was seized by an obscure dread. He tried to cry out but felt a rough hand grab him round the throat. Instinctively, like an animal defending itself, he pulled himself up on to his knees, clutching at the side of the boat. He struggled like that for a few seconds.

"Thérèse! Thérèse!" he called out in a muffled, rasping voice.

The young woman looked on, holding on to one of the seats with both hands as the boat creaked and danced on the river. She was unable to close her eyes, for a fearful muscular contraction kept them wide open, riveted on the horrific spectacle of the struggle. She was rigid and speechless.

"Thérèse! Thérèse!" the unfortunate Camille called again, now at his last gasp.

At his final appeal for help Thérèse burst into tears. Her nerve had broken, and the crisis that she had been dreading flung her trembling into the bottom of the boat. There she lay, collapsed in a heap and half dead.

Laurent was still shaking Camille and squeezing him by the throat. He eventually managed to wrench him away from the boat with his other hand, and held him up in the air like a child in his powerful, outstretched arms. As his head was thrown back and the neck unprotected, his victim, crazed with rage and terror, twisted round and sank his teeth into it. Then the murderer, stifling a howl of pain, flung the clerk into the river, but the teeth took with them a lump of his flesh.

Camille fell into the water with a scream.

Émile Zola

BEHIND THE WALL: A JOURNEY THROUGH CHINA

I walked isolated in whiteness through a forest of rain-dripping trees. Beneath my feet the stone stairway vanished upwards into air, and the land on either side seemed to fade into an abyss. I passed porters carrying atrocious loads of bricks and vegetables. They fell behind in mist, as if I had dreamed them. I could not tell how high the peaks loomed above me. Only occasionally, out of the whiteness where I thought the sun might hang, a ghostly file of pines would emerge, or a shoulder of grey stone.

The sacred way was almost derelict. A motley of booths and shacks lined it with walls of matted straw and tarpaulin roofs. Some still sold food and herbal medicine to passers-by, but most stood deserted. In others, a few pilgrims and hardy sightseers were slumped on rain-streaked benches, mud oozing underfoot, or were eating egg and noodles served from charred stoves, with the clouds swirling in.

After five hours I reached the temple dedicated to the mountain's protector, Puxian, embodiment of universal light.

Where almost everything else had been cleaned away by fire, his statue had survived here for a thousand years, and when I saw it I realised why. He rode a sixty ton life-size elephant in copper and bronze. Its columnar feet were planted foursquare on bronze lotus-pads. In its saddle Puxian was perched close beneath the temple's dome and gazed down from the dimness with an epicene beauty. At every solstice, it is said, the sun shines through a perforation in the cupola and strikes the jewel on the god's forehead. But now only a few monks presided beneath, looking crushed and old in their worn leggings and outsize boots.

Beyond, the way was a stone ladder into clouds. Around it the trees stood colourless and delicate – stencilled in pearl or washed away to tracings on the opaque air. In this invisible forest, I heard birdsong and pilgrims calling to one another. Almost unnoticeably, it began to rain. It fell with a vaporous quietness: I was climbing in its cloud. When I paused, I could hear it dripping unseen in the forest. The only movement was the quiver of the struck bamboo-stems, and the soundless fall of leaves, one by one, onto the earth.

Colin Thubron

ONE BY ONE IN THE DARKNESS

For now when she lay longing for sleep, a different image unrolled inexorably in her mind, repeated constantly, like a loop of film but sharper than that, more vivid, and running at just a fraction of a second slower than normal time, which gave it the heavy feel of a nightmare.

But this was no dream: she saw her father sitting at Lucy's kitchen table, drinking tea out of a blue mug. She could smell the smoke of his cigarette, even smell the familiar tweed of his jacket. He was talking through to Lucy, who was working out in the back scullery: she'd been doing the dishes when he arrived, and he told her to carry on with what she was about. He glanced up at the clock and said, "I wonder what's keeping Brian that he's not home yet," and Lucy replied, "There's a car pulled up outside now, but it's not Brian's, by the sound of it." And as soon as she spoke these words he heard her scream, as two men burst into the back scullery, and knocked her to the ground as they pushed past her; and then Helen's father saw them himself as they came into the kitchen, two men in parkas with the hoods pulled up, Halloween masks on their faces. He saw the guns, too, and he knew what they were going to do to him. The sound of a chair scraping back on the tiles, "Ah no, Christ Jesus no," and then they shot him at point-blank range, blowing half his head away. As they ran out of the house, one of them punched the air and whooped, because it had been so easy.

And at this point, in an abrupt reversal of the gentle descent of her childhood, Helen's vision swung violently away, and now she was aware of the cold light of dead stars; the graceless immensity of a dark universe. Now her image of her father's death was infinitely small, infinitely tender: the searing grief came from the tension between that smallness and the enormity of infinite time and space. No pity, no forgiveness, no justification: maybe if she could have conceived of a consciousness where every unique horror in the history of humanity was known and grieved for, it would have given her some comfort. Sometimes she felt that all she had was her grief, a grief she could scarcely bear.

In the solid stone house, the silence was uncanny.

One by one in the darkness, the sisters slept.

Deirdre Madden

CAPTAIN CORELLI'S MANDOLIN

I sit here and remember former times. I remember music in the night, and I know that all my joys have been pulled out of my mouth like teeth. I shall be hungry and thirsty and longing forever. If only I had a child, a child to suckle at the breast, if I had Antonio. I have been eaten up like bread. I lie down in thorns and my well is filled with stones. All my happiness was smoke.

O my poor father, silent and still, wasted and lost forever. My own father, who brought me up alone and taught me, who explained everything and took my hand and walked with me. Never again will I see your face, and in the morning you will not wake me. Never again in our ruined house will I see you sit, writing, always writing, your pipe clenched between your teeth and your sharp eyes shining. O my poor father who never tired of healing, who could not heal himself and died without his daughter; my throat aches from the hour you died alone.

I remain upon these piles of shattered rocks and imagine how it was. I remember Velisarios heaving away the tiles and beams as though it were his own father dead beneath them. And I remember when he brought my father out, covered in white dust, his head hanging back in Velisarios' arms, his mouth hanging open, his limbs all limp and dangling. I remember when Velisarios set him down and I knelt beside him, blind and drunk with tears, and I cradled his bloodied head in my hands and saw that his eyes were empty. His old eyes, looking not on me but on the hidden world beyond. And I thought then for the first time how thin and frail he was, how beaten and betrayed, and I realised that without his soul he was so light and thin that even I could lift him. And I raised up his body and clasped his head in my breast, and a great cry came out that must have been mine, and I saw as clearly as one sees a mountain that he was the only man I've loved who loved me to the end, and never bruised my heart and never for a single moment failed me.

Louis de Bernières

SPRING TORRENTS

Herr Klueber began by introducing himself. In the process, he bowed from the waist with such nobility of manner, while at the same time bringing one leg close to the other in so agreeable a fashion, and touching his heels together with such courtesy, that everyone was bound to think: "This man's linen and spiritual virtues are both of the first quality." The grooming of his exposed right hand, which he offered to Sanin modestly but firmly, exceeded the bounds of all probability: each single fingernail was a model of perfection. (In his left hand, which was clad in a suede glove, he held his hat which shone like a looking-glass: in the depths of the hat lay the other glove.) He then declared, in the choicest German phrases, that he desired to express his respect and his gratitude to the *Herr Auslaender* who had rendered so important a service to his future kinsmen, the brother of his betrothed. At this point, he gestured with his left hand, which held the hat, in the direction of Emil. The boy was evidently embarrassed, and turned away towards the window, putting his finger in his mouth. Herr Klueber added that he would count himself happy if he ever found it in his power to do something on his part that might be agreeable to the *Herr Auslaender.*

Sanin replied, in German, not without some difficulty, that he was most gratified... that his services had been of the most trivial nature... and invited his guests to be seated. Herr Klueber thanked him, and in an instant flung asunder his coat-tails and let himself down in a chair, but let himself down so lightly, and adhered to the chair so insecurely, that the inference was clear to all: this man only sat down out of politeness, and will immediately take wing once again. And indeed he leapt up instantly and executed a few modest movements with his legs, rather like some dance sequence. He then declared that, much to his regret, he could stay no longer since he was in a hurry to return to his shop – business before pleasure! But tomorrow was Sunday, and with the consent of Frau Lenore and Fräulein Gemma he had arranged a pleasurable excursion to Soden, to which he had the honour of inviting the *Herr Auslaender*. He expressed the hope that the distinguished foreigner would not refuse to grace the party with his presence. Sanin consented to grace the excursion with his presence. Thereupon Herr Klueber once again took his leave and departed – displaying a most agreeable glimpse of pea-green trousers of a most delicate hue, and emitting an equally delectable squeak from the soles of his brand new boots.

Ivan Turgenev

LICENTIATE TEACHERS' DIPLOMA

THE QUESTION

I dream'd that, as I wander'd by the way,
    Bare Winter suddenly was changed to Spring;
And gentle odours led my steps astray,
    Mix'd with a sound of waters murmuring
Along a shelving bank of turf, which lay
    Under a copse, and hardly dared to fling
Its green arms round the bosom of the stream,
But kiss'd it and then fled, as thou mightest in dream.

There grew pied wind-flowers and violets;
    Daisies, those pearl'd Arcturi of the earth,
The constellated flower that never sets;
    Faint oxlips; tender bluebells, at whose birth
The sod scarce heaved; and that tall flower that wets –
    Like a child, half in tenderness and mirth –
Its mother's face with heaven-collected tears
When the low wind, its playmate's voice, it hears.

And in the warm hedge grew lush eglantine,
    Green cowbind and the moonlight-colour'd May,
And cherry-blossoms, and white cups whose wine
    Was the bright dew yet drain'd not by the day;
And wild roses, and ivy serpentine,
    With its dark buds and leaves wandering astray;
And flowers, azure, black, and streak'd with gold,
Fairer than any waken'd eyes behold.

And nearer to the river's trembling edge
    There grew broad flag-flowers, purple prank'd with white
And starry river-buds among the sedge,
    And floating water-lilies, broad and bright,

Which lit the oak that overhung the hedge
  With moonlight beams of their own watery light;
And bulrushes, and reeds of such deep green
As soothed the dazzled eye with sober sheen.

Methought that of these visionary flowers
  I made a nosegay, bound in such a way
That the same hues which in their natural bowers
  Were mingled or opposed, the like array
Kept these imprison'd children of the Hours
  Within my hand; — and then, elate and gay,
I hasten'd to the spot whence I had come,
That I might there present it — O! to whom?

Percy Bysshe Shelley

TALES FROM OVID

Last comes the Age of Iron.
And the day of Evil dawns.
Modesty,
Loyalty,
Truth,
Go up like a mist — a morning sigh off a graveyard.

Snares, tricks, plots come hurrying
Out of their dens in the atom.
Violence is an extrapolation
Of the cutting edge
Into the orbit of the smile.
Now comes the love of gain — a new god
Made out of the shadow
Of all the others. A god who peers
Grinning from the roots of the eye-teeth.

Now sails bulged and the cordage cracked
In winds that still bewildered the pilots.
And the long trunks of trees
That had never shifted in their lives
From some mountain fastness
Leapt in their coffins
From wavetop to wavetop,
Then out over the rim of the unknown.

Meanwhile the ground, formerly free to all
As the air or sunlight,
Was portioned by surveyors into patches,
Between boundary markers, fences, ditches.

Earth's natural plenty no longer sufficed.
Man tore open the earth, and rummaged in her bowels.
Precious ores the Creator had concealed
As close to hell as possible
Were dug up – a new drug
For the criminal. So now iron comes
With its cruel ideas. And gold
With crueller. Combined, they bring war –
War, insatiable for the one,
With bloody hands employing the other.
Now man lives only by plunder. The guest
Is booty for the host. The bride's father,
Her heirloom, is a windfall piggybank
For the groom to shatter. Brothers
Who ought to love each other
Prefer to loathe. The husband longs
To bury his wife and she him.
Stepmothers, for the sake of their stepsons,
Study poisons. And sons grieve
Over their father's obdurate good health.

The inward ear, attuned to the Creator,
Is underfoot like a dog's turd. Astraea,
The Virgin
Of Justice — the incorruptible
Last of the immortals —
Abandons the blood-fouled earth.

Ted Hughes

THE DEATH OF THE BIRD

For every bird there is this last migration:
Once more the cooling year kindles her heart;
With a warm passage to the summer station
Love pricks the course in lights across the chart.

Year after year a speck on the map, divided
By a whole hemisphere, summons her to come;
Season after season, sure and safely guided,
Going away she is also coming home.

And being home, memory becomes a passion
With which she feeds her brood and straws her nest,
Aware of ghosts that haunt the heart's possession
And exiled love mourning within the breast.

The sands are green with a mirage of valleys;
The palm tree casts a shadow not its own;
Down the long architrave of temple or palace
Blows a cool air from moorland scraps of stone.

And day by day the whisper of love grows stronger;
That delicate voice, more urgent with despair,
Custom and fear constraining her no longer,
Drives her at last on the waste leagues of air.

A vanishing speck in those inane dominions,
Single and frail, uncertain of her place,
Alone in the bright host of her companions,
Lost in the blue unfriendliness of space.

She feels it close now, the appointed season:
The invisible thread is broken as she flies;
Suddenly, without warning, without reason,
The guiding spark of instinct winks and dies.

Try as she will, the trackless world delivers
No way, the wilderness of light no sign,
The immense and complex map of hills and rivers
Mocks her small wisdom with its vast design.

And darkness rises from the eastern valleys,
And the winds buffer her with their hungry breath,
And the great earth, with neither grief nor malice,
Receives the tiny burden of her death.

A. D. Hope

PRELUDES

I

The winter evening settles down
With smell of steaks in passageways.
Six o'clock.
The burnt-out ends of smoky days.
And now a gusty shower wraps
The grimy scraps
Of withered leaves about your feet
And newspapers from vacant lots;

The showers beat
On broken blinds and chimney-pots,
And at the corner of the street
A lonely cab-horse steams and stamps.

And then the lighting of the lamps.

II

The morning comes to consciousness
Of faint stale smells of beer
From the sawdust-trampled street
With all its muddy feet that press
To early coffee-stands.

With the other masquerades
That time resumes,
One thinks of all the hands
That are raising dingy shades
In a thousand furnished rooms.

III

You tossed a blanket from the bed,
You lay upon your back, and waited;
You dozed, and watched the night revealing
The thousand sordid images
Of which your soul was constituted;
They flickered against the ceiling.
And when all the world came back
And the light crept up between the shutters
And you heard the sparrows in the gutters,
You had such a vision of the street

As the street hardly understands;
Sitting along the bed's edge, where
You curled the papers from your hair,
Or clasped the yellow soles of feet
In the palms of both soiled hands.

IV

His soul stretched tight across the skies
That fade behind a city block,
Or trampled by insistent feet
At four and five and six o'clock;
And short square fingers stuffing pipes,
And evening newspapers, and eyes
Assured of certain certainties,
The conscience of a blackened street
Impatient to assume the world.

I am moved by fancies that are curled
Around these images, and cling:
The notion of some infinitely gentle
Infinitely suffering thing.

Wipe your hands across your mouth, and laugh;
The worlds revolve like ancient women
Gathering fuel in vacant lots.

T. S. Eliot

THE BAT

Castellated, tall
From battlements fall
Shades on heroic
Lonely grass,
Where the moonlight's echoes die and pass.
Near the rustic boorish,
Fustian Moorish,
Castle wall of the ultimate Shade,
With his cloak castellated as that wall, afraid,
The mountebank doctor,
The old stage quack,
Where decoy duck dust
Began to clack,
Watched Heliogabalusene the Bat
In his furred cloak hang head down from the flat
Wall, cling to what is convenient,
Lenient.
"If you hang upside down with squeaking shrill,
You will see dust, lust, and the will to kill,
And life is a matter of which way falls
Your tufted turreted Shade near these walls.
For muttering guttering shadow will plan
If you're ruined wall, or pygmy man,"
Said Heliogabalusene, "or a pig,
Or the empty Caesar in tall periwig."
And the mounteback doctor,
The old stage quack,
Spread out a black membraned wing of his cloak
And his shuffling footsteps seem to choke,
Near the Castle wall of the ultimate Shade
Where decoy duck dust
Quacks, clacks, afraid.

Edith Sitwell

TO MISS BLOUNT
EPISTLES TO THE SAME
On her leaving the town after the coronation

As some fond virgin, whom her mother's care
Drags from the town to wholesome country air,
Just when she learns to roll a melting eye,
And hear a spark, yet think no danger nigh;
From the dear man unwilling she must sever,
Yet takes one kiss before she parts for ever:
Thus from the world fair Zephalinda flew,
Saw others happy, and with sighs withdrew;
Not that their pleasures caused her discontent,
She sigh'd not that they stay'd, but that she went.

　　She went to plain-work, and to purling brooks,
Old-fashion'd halls, dull aunts, and croaking rooks:
She went from opera, park, assembly, play,
To morning walks, and prayers three hours a day;
To part her time 'twixt reading and bohea,
To muse, and spill her solitary tea,
Or o'er cold coffee trifle with the spoon,
Count the slow clock, and dine exact at noon;
Divert her eyes with pictures in the fire,
Hum half a tune, tell stories to the 'squire;
Up to her godly garret after seven,
There starve and pray, for that's the way to Heaven.

　　Some 'squire, perhaps, you take delight to rack;
Whose game is whisk, whose treat a toast in sack;
Who visits with a gun, presents you birds,
Then gives a smacking buss and cries, – No words!
Or with his hound comes hallooing from the stable,
Makes love with nods, and knees beneath a table;
Whose laughs are hearty, though his jests are coarse,
And loves you best of all things – but his horse.

In some fair ev'ning, on your elbow laid,
You dream of triumphs in the rural shade;
In pensive thought recall the fancied scene,
See coronations rise on ev'ry green;
Before you pass th' imaginary sights
Of lords, and earls, and dukes, and garter'd knights,
While the spread fan o'ershades your closing eyes;
Then give one flirt, and all the vision flies.
Thus vanish sceptres, coronets, and balls,
And leave you in lone woods, or empty walls!

Alexander Pope

NALLUR*

It's there,
   beneath the fallen fronds,
dry crackling
piles of broken twigs abandoned
wells of brackish
water lonely dunes
   it's there
the shadows of long bodies shrunk
in death
the leeching sun has drunk their
blood and
bloated swells among the piling
clouds
      it's there,
          death,
             smell it
in the air
its odour rank with sun and
thickening blood
mingling with fragrance from the

* The site of the largest and best known Hindu Temple in the Jaffna
  Peninsula in northern Sri Lanka.

frothy toddy
pots mingling like lolling heads from
blackened gibbets,
              it's there
                   amid the
clangour of
the temple bells, the clapping
hands, the brassy clash of cymbals,
         the zing of bullets
         cries of death
         drowned in the roar
         of voices calling
         Skanda
         by his thousand
         names
         Murugan, Kartikkeya
         Arumugam............
"We pray, we cry, we clamour
oh Sri Kumaran, be not like the god
Who does not hear, deaf
Sandesveran,"
Thirtham now no longer nectar of
the gods
brims over but is bitter, bitter,
And at the entrance to Nallur
the silent guns are trained
upon a faceless terror

Outside,
         The landscape
changes
the temples by the shore are
smoking
ruins charred stone blackened,
on empty roads are strewn

the debris of warfare,
Stained discarded dressings
burnt out abandoned vehicles
a trail of blood
Soon mopped up by the thirsty sun
Turned away from bloody
skirmishes
of humankind, the gods are blinded
by the rain of bullets,
Six faced Arumugam
all twelve eyes
Close in darkness

The land is empty now
the pitted limestone
invaded by the sea
drowns, vanishes,
waves of rust swell and billow
beating into hollow caves and burial
urns
filled with the ash of bodies
Cremated by the fire of bullets.

Jean Arasanayagam

SOCIAL GRACE

I expect you've heard this a million times before
But I absolutely adored your last play
I went four times — and now to think
that here I am actually talking to you!
It's thrilling! Honestly it is, I mean,
It's always thrilling isn't it to meet someone really
    celebrated?
I mean someone who really does things.

I expect all this is a terrible bore for you.
After all you go everywhere and know everybody.
It must be wonderful to go absolutely everywhere
And know absolutely everybody and − Oh dear −
Then to have to listen to someone like me,
I mean someone absolutely ordinary just one of your public.
No-one will believe me when I tell them
That I have actually been talking to the great man himself.
It must be wonderful to be so frightfully brainy
And know all the things that you know
I'm not brainy a bit, neither is my husband,
Just plain humdrum, that's what we are.
But we do come up to town occasionally
And go to shows and things. Actually my husband
Is quite a critic, not professionally of course,
What I mean is that he isn't all that easily pleased.
He doesn't like everything. Oh no not by any means.
He simply hated that thing at the Haymarket
Which everybody went on about. "Rubbish" he said,
Straight out like that, "Damned Rubbish!"
I nearly died because heaps of people were listening.
But that's quite typical of him. He just says what he thinks.
And he can't stand all this highbrow stuff −
Do you know what I mean? − All these plays about people
    being miserable
And never getting what they want and not even committing
    suicide
But just being absolutely wretched. He says he goes to the
    theatre
To have a good time. That's why he simply loves all your
    things,
    I mean they relax him and he doesn't have to think.
And he certainly does love a good laugh.

You should have seen him the other night when we went to
    that film
With what's-her-name in it – I can't remember the title.
I thought he'd have a fit, honestly I did.
You must know the one I mean, the one about the man
    who comes home
And finds his wife has been carrying on with his best friend
And of course he's furious at first then he decides to
    teach her a lesson.
You must have seen it. I wish I could remember the name
But that's absolutely typical of me, I've got a head like a
    sieve,
I keep on forgetting things and as for names – well!
I just cannot for the life of me remember them.
Faces yes, I never forget a face because I happen to be
    naturally observant
And always have been since I was a tiny kiddie
But names – Oh dear! I'm quite hopeless.
I feel such a fool sometimes
I do honestly.

Noël Coward

THE CHRONICLES OF CLOVIS

"And do you really ask us to believe," Sir Wilfred was saying, "that you have discovered a means for instructing animals in the art of human speech, and that dear old Tobermory has proved your first successful pupil?"

"It is a problem at which I have worked for the last seventeen years," said Mr Appin, "but only during the last eight or nine months have I been rewarded with glimmerings of success. Of course I have experimented with thousands of animals, but latterly only with cats, those wonderful creatures which have assimilated themselves so marvellously with our civilisation while retaining all their highly developed feral instincts. Here and there among cats one comes across an outstanding superior intellect, just as one does among the ruck of human beings, and when I made the acquaintance of Tobermory a week ago I saw at once that I was in contact with a 'Beyond-cat' of extraordinary intelligence. I had gone far along the road to success in recent experiments; with Tobermory, as you call him, I have reached the goal."

Mr Appin concluded his remarkable statement in a voice which he strove to divest of a triumphant inflection. No-one said "Rats," though Clovis's lips moved in a monosyllabic contortion which probably invoked those rodents of disbelief.

"And do you mean to say," asked Miss Resker, after a slight pause, "that you have taught Tobermory to say and understand easy sentences of one syllable?"

"My dear Miss Resker," said the wonder-worker patiently, "one teaches little children and savages and backward adults in that piecemeal fashion; when one has once solved the problem of making a beginning with an animal of highly developed intelligence one has no need for those halting methods. Tobermory can speak our language with perfect correctness."

This time Clovis very distinctly said, "Beyond-rats!" Sir Wilfred was more polite, but equally sceptical.

"Hadn't we better have the cat in and judge for ourselves?" suggested Lady Blemley.

Sir Wilfred went in search of the animal, and the company settled themselves down to the languid expectation of witnessing some more or less adroit drawing-room ventriloquism.

In a minute Sir Wilfred was back in the room, his face white beneath its tan and his eyes dilated with excitement.

"By Gad, it's true!"

H. H. Munro (Saki)

BIRDSONG

Stephen sat opposite Isabelle in the train going south towards Soissons and Reims. He felt the simple elation of his victory, the fact that it was he who had won, who had persuaded Isabelle against the weight of convention and sound argument to do the difficult and dangerous thing. And there was the deeper happiness of being with this woman, whom he loved, and the undeniable evidence, for the first time, that she was his. Isabelle smiled, then shook her head incredulously from side to side with closed eyes. When she opened them again they had a look of resignation.

"What will they say? What will he say to Bérard and to his friends?" Her voice was intrigued but not anxious.

"It's not the first time a wife has left her husband." Stephen had no idea what Azaire would say, but he did not feel inclined to imagine. He felt it was important that he and Isabelle concentrated on themselves.

The train was the last of the evening, so they had had little choice of destination. At the station Isabelle had wrapped a shawl over her face, fearing recognition as she clambered onto the train. As it made its way south over the flat landscape, she relaxed; there might be years of regret, but the prospect of immediate drama and reverse had gone.

The train stopped at a dimly lit station and they looked out of the window at a porter unloading mail and pushing a trolley full of boxes to a wooden building that gave on to the empty stockyard. The man's face showed pale in the darkness. Behind him was the ordered black swell of a street, leading uphill into a town where the occasional yellow light showed hazily from behind curtains and shutters.

The train shrugged and clanked out of the station and made its way south through the tranquil night. The summer was almost at an end and there was an edge of cold to the air. To the east was the forest of Ardennes, and beyond it the Rhine. After a stop at Reims they followed the line of the Marne through Joinville. Occasionally the gloomy river would be caught by moonlight when the railway travelled alongside before retaking its own course through cuttings and embankments whose high sides enclosed it in darkness.

As they moved south, Isabelle came and sat next to Stephen, resting her head against his body. The rolling motion of the train made her eyes heavy; she slept as it picked out its set course, nosing its way south where the Marne joined the river Meuse, whose course linked Sedan to Verdun – a flat, unargued path through the lowlands of her native country.

She dreamed of pale faces beneath rose-coloured lights; Lisette at the corner of the stairs, the bloodless features in the red glow, a lost girl, and others like her caught in some repeated loop of time, its pattern enforced by the rhythmic motion of the train; many white-skinned faces with dark eyes, staring in disbelief.

Sebastian Faulks

THE MIRROR OF THE SEA

The love that is given to ships is profoundly different from the love men feel for every other work of their hands — the love they bear to their houses, for instance — because it is untainted by the pride of possession. The pride of skill, the pride of responsibility, the pride of endurance there may be, but otherwise it is a disinterested sentiment. No seaman ever cherished a ship, even if she belonged to him, merely because of the profit she put in his pocket. No-one, I think, ever did; for a ship-owner, even of the best, has always been outside the pale of that sentiment embracing in a feeling of intimate, equal fellowship the ship and the man, backing each other against the implacable, if sometimes dissembled, hostility of their world of waters. The sea — this truth must be confessed — has no generosity. No display of manly qualities — courage, hardihood, endurance, faithfulness — has ever been known to touch its irresponsible consciousness of power. The ocean has the conscienceless temper of a savage autocrat spoiled by much adulation. He cannot brook the slightest appearance of defiance, and has remained the irreconcilable enemy of ships and men ever since ships and men had the unheard-of audacity to go afloat together in the face of his frown. From that day he has gone on swallowing up fleets and men without his resentment being glutted by the number of victims — by so many wrecked ships and wrecked lives. Today, as ever, he is ready to beguile and betray, to smash and to drown the incorrigible optimism of men who, backed by the fidelity of ships, are trying to wrest from him the fortune of their house, the dominion of their world, or only a dole of food for their hunger. If not always in the hot mood to smash, he is always stealthily ready for a drowning. The most amazing wonder of the deep is its unfathomable cruelty.

Joseph Conrad

THE ENGLISH PATIENT

It was sometime after this that she had come across the English patient – someone who looked like a burned animal, taut and dark, a pool for her. And now, months later, he is her last patient in the Villa San Girolamo, their war over, both of them refusing to return with the others to the safety of the Pisa hospitals. All the coastal ports, such as Sorrento and Marina di Pisa, are now filled with North American and British troops waiting to be sent home. But she washed her uniform, folded it and returned it to the departing nurses. The war is not over everywhere, she was told. The war is over. This war is over. The war here. She was told it would be like desertion. This is not desertion. I will stay here. She was warned of the uncleared mines and lack of water and food. She came upstairs to the burned man, the English patient, and told him she would stay as well.

He said nothing, unable even to turn his head towards her, but his fingers slipped into her white hand, and when she bent forward to him he put his dark fingers into her hair and felt it cool within the valley of his fingers.

How old are you?

Twenty.

There was a duke, he said, who when he was dying wanted to be carried halfway up the tower in Pisa so he could die looking out into the middle distance.

A friend of my father's wanted to die while Shanghai-dancing. I don't know what it is. He had just heard of it himself.

What does your father do?

He is... he is in the war.

You're in the war too.

She does not know anything about him. Even after a month or so of caring for him and allotting him the needles of morphine. There was shyness at first within both of them, made more evident by the fact that they were now alone. Then it was suddenly overcome. The patients and doctors and nurses and equipment and sheets and towels – all went back down the hill into Florence and then to Pisa. She had salted away codeine tablets, as well as the morphine. She watched the departures, the line of trucks. Goodbye, then. She waved from his window, bringing the shutters to a close.

Michael Ondaatje

A ROOM OF ONE'S OWN

Dinner was being served in the great dining hall. Far from being spring it was in fact an evening in October. Everybody was assembled in the big dining-room. Dinner was ready. Here was the soup. It was a plain gravy soup. There was nothing to stir the fancy in that. One could have seen through the transparent liquid any pattern that there might have been on the plate itself. But there was no pattern. The plate was plain. Next came beef with its attendant greens and potatoes – a homely trinity, suggesting the rumps of cattle in a muddy market, and sprouts curled and yellowed at the edge, and bargaining and cheapening and women with string bags on Monday morning. There was no reason to complain of human nature's daily food, seeing that the supply was sufficient and coal miners doubtless were sitting down to less. Prunes and custard followed. And if anyone complains that prunes, even when mitigated by custard, are an uncharitable vegetable (fruit they are not), stringy as a miser's heart and exuding a fluid such as might run in misers' veins who have denied themselves wine and warmth for eighty years and yet not given to the poor, he should reflect that there are people whose charity embraces even the prune. Biscuits and cheese came next, and here the water jug was liberally passed round, for it is the nature of biscuits to be dry, and these were biscuits to the core. That was all. The meal was over. Everybody scraped their chairs back; the swing doors swung violently to and fro; soon the hall was emptied of every sign of food and made ready no doubt for breakfast next morning. Down corridors and up staircases the youth of England went banging and singing. And was it for a guest, a stranger (for I had no more right here in Fernham than in Trinity or Somerville or Girton or Newnham or Christchurch), to say, "The dinner was not good," or to say (we were now, Mary Seton and I, in her sitting room), "Could we not have dined up here alone?" for if I had said anything of the kind I should have been prying and searching into the secret economies of a house which to the stranger wears so fine a front of gaiety and courage. No, one could say nothing of the sort. Indeed, conversation for a moment flagged. The human frame being what it is, heart, body and brain all mixed together, and not contained in separate compartments as they will be no doubt in another million years, a good dinner is of great importance to good talk. One cannot think well, love well, sleep well, if one has not dined well.

Virginia Woolf

EUGÉNIE GRANDET

Expected misfortunes nearly always happen. At that moment, Nanon, Madame Grandet, and Eugénie, who could not think of the old cooper's return without a shudder, heard the sound of a familiar knock.

"That's papa," said Eugénie.

She took away the saucer of sugar, leaving a few lumps on the tablecloth. Nanon removed the egg plate. Madame

Grandet started up like a frightened deer. It was a moment of complete panic that amazed Charles, who could not understand it.

"But what's the matter?" he asked.

"My father's coming," said Eugénie.

"What of it?..."

Monsieur Grandet came in, looked straight at the table and at Charles; he took in everything.

"Aha, you've made a party for your nephew; that's fine, very fine, indeed very fine," he said without stammering. "When the cat's away, the mice will play."

"A party?..." thought Charles, quite unable to conceive the slightest idea of the diet and customs of this household.

"Give me my glass, Nanon," said the miser.

Eugénie brought the glass. Grandet took from his pocket a horn-handled knife with a large blade, cut a slice of bread, took a little butter, spread it carefully, and began to eat standing up. At that moment, Charles was putting sugar in his coffee. Père Grandet noticed the sugarlumps, looked closely at his wife, who turned pale, and took three steps forward. He leaned over and whispered into the poor woman's ear, "Where did you get all that sugar from?"

"Nanon went to Fessard's for it; we didn't have any."

It is impossible to imagine the profound concern aroused in the three women by this scene, enacted without a word. Nanon had left her kitchen and was looking into the room to see what would happen. Charles tasted his coffee and, finding it too bitter, looked for the sugar, which Grandet had already put away.

"What are you looking for, nephew?" he asked.

"The sugar."

"Put some milk in, that will sweeten your coffee," replied the master of the house.

Eugénie brought back the saucer of sugar that Grandet had already put away, and placed it on the table, looking calmly at her father. The Parisian girl who, to help her lover escape, takes the weight of a silken ladder on her weak arms, certainly shows no more courage that Eugénie did in putting the sugar back on the table. The lover will reward the Parisian girl, who will proudly display a beautiful bruised arm, but every bruise will be bathed in tears and kisses and cured by love. Charles, however, would never know the secret of the deep emotions which were breaking his cousin's heart as she stood devastated by the old cooper's look.

Honoré de Balzac

GOOD BEHAVIOUR

Gulls' Cry, where Mummie and I live now, is built on the edge of a cliff. Its windows lean out over the deep anchorage of the boat cove like bosoms on an old ship's figurehead. Sometimes I think (though I would never say it) how nice that bosoms are alright to have now; in the twenties when I grew up I used to tie them down with a sort of binder. Bosoms didn't do then. They didn't do at all. Now, it's too late for mine.

I like to sing when nobody can hear me and put me off the note. I sang that day as I went upstairs. Our kitchen and dining-room are on the lowest level of this small Gothic folly of a house. The stairs, with their skimpy iron banister, bring you up to the hall and the drawing-room, where I put all our mementoes of Papa when we moved here from Temple Alice. The walls are papered in pictures and photographs of him riding winners. Silver cups stand in rows on the chimney-piece, not to mention the model of a seven-pound sea trout and several rather misty snapshots of bags of grouse laid out on the steps of Temple Alice.

Mummie never took any proper interest in this gallery, and when her heart got so dicky, and I converted the room into a charming bed-sit for her, she seemed to turn her eyes away from everything she might have remembered with love and pleasure. One knows sick people and old people can be difficult and unrewarding, however much one does for them: not exactly ungrateful, just absolutely maddening. But I enjoy the room whenever I go in. It's all my own doing and Mummie, lying back in her nest of pretty pillows, is my doing too — I insist on her being scrupulously clean and washed and scented.

"Luncheon," I said cheerfully, the tray I carried making a lively rattle. "Shall I sit you up a bit?" She was lying down among her pillows as if she were sinking through the bed. She never makes an effort for herself. That comes of having me.

"I don't feel very hungry," she said. A silly remark. I know she always pretends she can't eat and when I go out makes Rose do her fried eggs and buttered toast and all the things the doctor says she mustn't touch.

"Smell that," I said, and lifted the cover off my perfect quenelles.

"I wonder if you'd pull down the blind" — not a word about the quenelles — "the sun's rather in my eyes."

"You really want the blind down?"

She nodded.

"All the way?"

"Please."

I went across then and settled her for her tray, pulling her up and putting a pillow in the exact spot behind her back, and another tiny one behind her head. She simply refused to look as if she felt comfortable. I'm used to that. I arranged the basket tray (straight from Harrods) across her, and put her luncheon tray on it.

"Now then," I said – one must be firm – "a delicious chicken mousse."

"Rabbit, I bet," she said.

Molly Keane

LOVE IN THE TIME OF CHOLERA

"None of that," said Lorenzo Daza, "This is a matter for men and it will be decided by men."

His tone had become threatening, and a customer who had just sat down at a nearby table turned to look at them. Florentino Ariza spoke in a most tenuous voice, but with the most imperious resolution of which he was capable:

"Be that as it may, I cannot answer without knowing what she thinks. It would be a betrayal."

Then Lorenzo Daza leaned back in his chair, his eyelids reddened and damp, and his left eye spun in its orbit and stayed twisted toward the outside. He, too, lowered his voice.

"Don't force me to shoot you," he said.

Florentino Ariza felt his intestines filling with cold froth. But his voice did not tremble because he felt himself illuminated by the Holy Spirit.

"Shoot me," he said, with his hand on his chest. "There is no greater glory than to die for love."

Lorenzo Daza had to look at him sideways, like a parrot, to see him with his twisted eye. He did not pronounce the four words so much as spit them out, one by one:

"Son of a bitch!"

That same week he took his daughter away on the journey that would make her forget. He gave no explanation at all, but burst into her bedroom, his mustache stained with fury and his chewed cigar, and ordered her to pack. She asked him where they were going, and he answered: "To our death."

Frightened by a response that seemed too close to the truth, she tried to face him with the courage of a few days before, but he took off his belt with its hammered copper buckle, twisted it around his fist, and hit the table with a blow that resounded through the house like a rifle shot. Fermina Daza knew very well the extent and occasion of her own strength, and so she packed a bedroll with two straw mats and a hammock, and two large trunks with all her clothes, certain that this was a trip from which she would never return. Before she dressed, she locked herself in the bathroom and wrote a brief farewell letter to Florentino Ariza on a sheet torn from the pack of toilet paper. Then she cut off her entire braid at the nape of her neck with cuticle scissors, rolled it inside a velvet box embroidered with gold thread, and sent it along with the letter.

Gabriel García Márquez

INDEX OF AUTHORS

INDEX OF TITLES

PUBLISHERS
of prose works from which selections
have been taken

GRADE FOUR

The Iron Woman by Ted Hughes: Faber & Faber Ltd
Flour Babies by Anne Fine: Penguin
Charlotte's Web by E. B. White: Puffin
Harry Potter and the Philosopher's Stone by J. K. Rowling:
    Bloomsbury
The Borrowers by Mary Norton: Puffin
The Wind in the Willows by Kenneth Grahame: Methuen
Peter Pan by J. M. Barrie: Oxford University Press
The Sheep-Pig by Dick King-Smith: Puffin

GRADE FIVE

Premlata and the Festival of Lights by Rumer Godden: Macmillan
Goodnight Mister Tom by Michelle Magorian: Puffin
Haroun and the Sea of Stories by Salman Rushdie: Penguin/Granta
    Books
Why The Whales Came by Michael Morpurgo: Collins/Mammoth
The Red Pony by John Steinbeck: Mammoth/Mandarin
The Indian in the Cupboard by Lynne Reid Banks: Lions
The Machine Gunners by Robert Westall: Macmillan
Mrs Frisby and the Rats of NIMH by Robert C. O'Brien: Puffin

GRADE SIX

The Daydreamer by Ian McEwan: Jonathan Cape/Vintage
The Call of the Wild by Jack London: Penguin Popular Classics
The Woman in Black by Susan Hill: Reed Consumer Books/
    Mandarin
The Village by the Sea by Anita Desai: Puffin
The Magician's Nephew by C. S. Lewis: Lions
Jane Eyre by Charlotte Bronte: Macmillan/Penguin
Roll of Thunder, Hear my Cry by Mildred D. Taylor: Puffin
The Hounds of the Morrigan by Pat O'Shea: Oxford University
    Press Children's Modern Classics

GRADE SEVEN
Northern Lights by Philip Pullman: Pointi Scholastic
Royal Jelly by Roald Dahl: Puffin
Red Sky in the Morning by Elizabeth Laird: Heinemann Educational
  Books Ltd
Walk Two Moons by Sharon Creech: Macmillan
The Secret by Ruth Thomas: Random House (Red Fox)
The Horla by Guy de Maupassant: Penguin
Watching the Watcher by Gaye Hiçyilmaz: Faber & Faber Ltd
The Wheel of Surya by Jamila Gavin: Methuen/Mammoth

GRADE EIGHT
A Child's Christmas in Wales by Dylan Thomas: Dolphin (Orion's
  Children's Books/Puffin)
Metamorphosis by Franz Kafka: Minerva
Lord of the Flies by William Golding: Faber & Faber Ltd
Far From the Madding Crowd by Thomas Hardy: Macmillan
The Great Gatsby by F. Scott Fitzgerald: Penguin
Emma by Jane Austen: Oxford University Press
Lord Arthur Saville's Crime by Oscar Wilde: Collins
Sophie's World by Jostein Gaarder: Dolphin

BRONZE MEDAL
Behind the Scenes at the Museum by Kate Atkinson: Black Swan
Silas Marner by George Eliot: Penguin
Angela's Ashes by Frank McCourt: Flamingo
How Green Was My Valley by Richard Llewellyn: Penguin
Fugitive Pieces by Anne Michaels: Bloomsbury
All the Pretty Horses by Cormac McCarthy: Picador
Old St Paul's by William Harrison Ainsworth: George Newes
Wives and Daughters by Elizabeth Gaskell: Oxford University Press

SILVER MEDAL
Paddy Clarke Ha Ha Ha by Roddy Doyle: Minerva
The God of Small Things by Arundhati Roy: Harper Collins/
  Flamingo
Great Expectations by Charles Dickens: Cambridge University
  Press

Lady's Maid by Margaret Forster: Penguin
Lucia in London by E. F. Benson: Penguin
Jill by Philip Larkin: Faber & Faber Ltd
The Lady of the Camellias by Alexander Dumas: Sutton Publishing
   (Pocket Classics)
The Last September by Elizabeth Bowen: Penguin

GOLD MEDAL

Thérèse Raquin by Émile Zola: Oxford University Press World
   Classics
Spring Torrents by Ivan Turgenev: Penguin
Writing Home by Alan Bennett: Faber & Faber Ltd
Our Man in Havana by Graham Greene: Penguin
The Magic Lantern by Ingmar Bergman: Penguin
Captain Corelli's Mandolin by Louis de Bernières: Minerva
Behind The Wall by Colin Thubron: Heinemann
One by One in the Darkness by Deirdre Madden: Faber & Faber Ltd

LICENTIATE TEACHERS' DIPLOMA

Good Behaviour by Molly Keane: Abacus Books
The Complete Saki by H. H. Munro (Saki): Penguin
Birdsong by Sebastian Faulks: Hutchinson
Eugénie Grandet by Honoré de Balzac: Oxford University Press
A Room of One's Own by Virginia Woolf: Harper Collins
The English Patient by Michael Ondaatje: Picador
Love in the Time of Cholera by Gabriel García Márquez: Penguin
The Mirror of the Sea : Joseph Conrad: Oxford University Press